Social Media at BBC News

"Valerie Belair-Gagnon has provided a ground-breaking analysis of the impact of social media on the practice of journalism. Her book's examination of the BBC offers a compelling look at how a global leader in journalism is adapting to the age of connected citizens."
—*John Pavlik, Rutgers University, USA*

"This book offers an important analysis of the practical and ethical issues for a global broadcaster embracing social media. It brings to life the opportunities and dilemmas for a traditional news organisation adapting to the open, collaborative digital age."
—*Richard Sambrook, Cardiff University*
(Former Director, BBC Global News)

"Valerie Belair-Gagnon's work on the BBC offers the defining work on the world's premiere public broadcast institution as it attempts to reckon with the rise of user-generated content. The text offers a fascinating detailing of the tensions between the institution's standards for accuracy and the new demands and perhaps uncertainty of verification for social media. Through intensive fieldwork, scholars and journalists alike should find an essential tale full of lessons from a formidable institution adapting to the social media age."
—*Nikki Usher, George Washington University, USA and*
author of Making News at The New York Times

Since the emergence of social media in the journalistic landscape, the BBC has sought to produce reporting more connected to its audience while retaining its authority as a public broadcaster in crisis reporting. Using empirical analysis of crisis news production at the BBC, this book shows that the emergence of social media at the BBC and the need to manage this kind of material led to a new media logic in which tech-savvy journalists take on a new centrality in the newsroom. In this changed context, the politico-economic and sociocultural logic have led to a more connected newsroom involving this new breed of journalists and BBC audience. This examination of news production events shows that in the midst of transformations in journalistic practices and norms—including newsgathering, sourcing, distribution, and impartiality—the BBC has reasserted its authority as a public broadcaster.

Valerie Belair-Gagnon is Research Scholar and Executive Director of the Information Society Project at Yale Law School. She has written on media, technologies, and law, drawing attention to the issues surrounding changes in technologies and media norms and practices.

Routledge Research in Journalism

Social Media at BBC News

The Re-Making of Crisis Reporting

Valerie Belair-Gagnon

Routledge
Taylor & Francis Group

LONDON AND NEW YORK

First published 2015 by Routledge

2 Park Square, Milton Park, Abingdon, Oxfordshire OX14 4RN
711 Third Avenue, New York, NY 10017

Routledge is an imprint of the Taylor & Francis Group,
an informa business

First issued in paperback 2017

Copyright © 2015 Taylor & Francis

Library of Congress Cataloging-in-Publication Data

Belair-Gagnon, Valerie.
   Social media at BBC news : the re-making of crisis reporting /
by Valerie Belair-Gagnon.
      pages cm. — (Routledge research in journalism ; 10)
   Includes bibliographical references and index.
   1. Television broadcasting of news—Great Britain.   2. Online
journalism—Great Britain—History—21st century.   3. Social
media—Political aspects—Great Britain.   4. British Broadcasting
Corporation.   I. Title.
   PN5124.T4B46   2015
   070.1'950941—dc23
   2014035592

ISBN: 978-1-138-82348-8 (hbk)
ISBN: 978-1-138-06714-1 (pbk)

Typeset in Sabon
by Apex CoVantage, LLC

To my parents, Mireille and Robert

Contents

Figures

Abbreviations

ABC	American Broadcasting Corporation
ABS-CNB	Alto Broadcasting System-Chronicle Broadcasting Network (South Korea)
ANI	Indian News Channel
AuBC	Australian Broadcasting Corporation
AVOD	Audio and video on demand (see VOD)
APTN	Associated Press Television News
ARD	Arbeitsgemeinschaft der öffentlich-rechtlichen Rundfunkanstalten der Bundesrepublik of Deutshland
AOL	America Online
ATV	Asia Television Limited, Cantonese television channel
BARB	Broadcasters' Audience Research Board (UK)
BBC	British Broadcasting Corporation
CBC	Canadian Broadcasting Corporation
CCTV	China Central Television
DAB	Digital Audio Broadcasting
DMCS	Department of Media Culture and Sports
EBU	European Broadcasting Union
ENEX	European News Exchange
FM&T	Future Media and Technologies
IBA	Independent Broadcasting Authority
IHA	Ihlas Haver Ajansi-Ihlas News Agency (a Turkish News Agency)
ITV	Independent Television
LWT	London Weekend Television
KBS	Korean Broadcasting System
MSN	The Microsoft Network
NASA	National Aeronautics and Space Administration
NHK	Japan Broadcasting Corporation
NTN	Nippon Television Network
PDP	Personal Digital Production
R-C	Radio-Canada
RPI	Retail Price Index

UGC	User-generated content
UK	United Kingdom
URL	Uniform Resource Locator
US (or USA)	United States
SBS	Special Broadcasting Service (Australia)
SBS	Seoul Broadcasting System
TBS	Tokyo Broadcasting System
TVC	BBC Television Centre (London)
TVNZ	Television New Zealand
VBS	Vietnamese Broadcasting Service Television
VOD	Video on Demand
VoIP	Voice over Internet Protocol
ZDF	Zweites Deutsches Fernsehen/Second German Television

Selected Social Media

Site	Description	URL
Audioboo	Audio content sharing.	www.audioboo.com
Bebo	Photos, videos, blogs, apps share between friends.	www.bebo.com
Delicious	Social bookmarking. Allows users to locate and save websites matching their interests.	www.delicious.com
Facebook	Photos, videos, blogs, apps share between friends.	www.facebook.com
Flickr	Photo sharing, comment, photo networking.	www.flickr.com
FourSquare	Location-based mobile social network.	www.foursquare.com
Google +	Photos, videos, blogs, apps share between users.	plus.google.com
Hotlist	Geo-social aggregator to know where users' friends are, were, and will be.	www.hotlist.com
Hootsuite	Management system for businesses and organisations to follow social networks from one web-based dashboard.	www.hootsuite.com
Iran.twazzup	Track tweets on Iran.	iran.twazzup.com
LinkedIn	Business and professional networking.	www.linkedin.com
MySpace	Social entertainment (video and audio).	www.myspace.com
Picassa	Picture sharing on Google.	picassa.google.com
PinInterest	Online pinboard for organising and sharing things users love.	www.pinterest.com
Projeqt	Online storytelling engine.	www.projeqt.com
Scribe	Content managing software.	www.scribe.com
Scoopit	Users curate stories on the web on a topic.	www.scoop.it

(*Continued*)

Site	Description	URL
Storyful	Helps newsrooms to discover and verify content on the social web.	www.storyful.com
Storify	Users curate story by way of social media.	www.storify.com
StumbleUpon	Stumble through websites that match users' selected interests.	www.stumbleupon.com
Tumblr	Blog and microblogging platform.	www.tumblr.com
Tweetminster	Tweets, shared stories, trends, and people in UK politics. Identifies network of experts and influencers on Twitter in finance and politics.	www.tweetminster.com
Tweetscan	Twitter and microblog search.	www.tweetscan.com
Twitpic	Photos and videos sharing.	www.twitpic.com
Twitter	Microblogging, RSS, updates.	www.twitter.com
Twitterfall	Twitter is queried from the Twitterfall server.	www.twitterfall.com
YouTube	Video sharing website.	www.youtube.com

Timeline

23 June 2004	Launch of the BBC Neil Report
26 December 2004	Asian Tsunami
7 July 2005	London bombings, which led to the creation of the UGC Hub and a 24/7-hour service, although pre-7/7 the UGC Hub was running as a pilot project
March 2006	Launch of White Paper, "A public service for all: BBC in the digital age"
25 April 2006	Launch of Creative Future, an editorial endeavour created to deliver more value to the audience
18 June 2007	Launch of the report "From seesaw to wagon wheel: Safeguarding impartiality in the 21st century"
August 2007	Burmese anti-government protests
2007–2008	BBC UGC Hub moves to the main multimedia newsroom
26 November 2008	Mumbai attacks and live-feed experience
2008	BBC updates its guidance and includes "social networking"
12 June 2009	Iran presidential election
November 2009	College of Journalism starts a one-day social media course called "Making the Web Work for You"
16 November 2009	Appointment of BBC Social Media Editor's Alex Gubbay
December 2009	Launch of BBC Academy (College of Journalism)
12 January 2010	Haiti earthquake and crowdsourcing
February 2010	BBC World Service Director Peter Horrocks tells staff "tweet or be sacked"
2010	BBC updates its guidance and includes "Twitter". Hashtag starts appearing on television
Winter 2011	The "Arab Spring"
2011	BBC integrates blogs into its news correspondent webpage
2 May 2011	Osama bin Laden's death
June 2011	Launch of BBC Twitter Guidelines

Acknowledgments

This book began its life in 2009 when I moved to London. I am thankful to all the people who made this journey enriching. I want to thank BBC News staff for opening up and letting me observe the newsroom during the Arab Spring of 2011, a time when the BBC experimented with new ways of reporting with social media. I want to particularly thank Grahame Davies; this research would not have been possible without his help. I want to also thank James Buchanan, John Curran, John Pavlik, Richard Sambrook, James Stevenson, and Jon Williams.

This book has been written in different settings. From 2009 to 2013, I enjoyed the academic and institutional support of City University London. I want to thank my PhD supervisor Professor Jean K. Chalaby and members of the committee, Stuart Allan and Suzanne Franks, for their time and advice. I am also thankful to colleagues and friends at City University London: Dimitri Akrivos, Rashid Aziz, Lena Karamanidou, John Kerr, Damien Lanfrey, Eugene McLaughlin, Dogus Simsek, Judith Townend, Brooke van Dam, and Frank Webster. Since July 2013, I have been fortunate to enjoy the academic community and institutional support of the Information Society Project at Yale Law School. I am grateful to Jack M. Balkin, Margot Kaminski, fellows, and staff for the support they have provided me to write this book. I also want to thank colleagues and friends: David L. Altheide, Daniel Bennett, Anupam Chanders, Danielle Citron, Robert Dingwall, Nikki Usher Layser, Hugh Meighen, Charles Miller, Jonathan Paquette, John V. Pavlik, Vincent Raynauld, Matthias Revers, Neil Richard, Emmanuelle Richez, Bryan Robert, Molly Sauter, Yeny Serrano, Julia Sonnevend, Daniel Strieff, and Francesca Taddeo.

Thank you to the following journalists who accepted to participate in this study: Paul Adam, Tim Awford, Kevin Bakhurst, Trushar Barot, Mark Blank-Settle, Peter Bowes, Tom Brook, Decland Carlam, Andy Carvin, John Conway, John Curran, Dr Grahame Davies, Richard Dawkins, John Dewitt, Jonny Dymond, Huw Edwards, Matthew Eltringham, Michelle Fleury, Jonathan Greenwood, Chris Hamilton, Pat Heery, Caroline Hepker, Colette Hume, Aled Huw, Jonathan Josephs, Jacky Martens, Janet Mcallen, Theresa Moon, Valerie Nazareth, Chris Parthridge, Guy Pelham, Steve

Phillips, Marek Pruszewicz, Paul Royall, Richard Sambrook, Abigail Sawyer, James Stevenson, Vicky Taylor, Ruth Thomas, Chris Walton, Claire Wardle, Jon Williams, and others. Thanks to Ariel Dobkin, Felisa Salvago-Keyes, and Kathleen Laurentiev.

I am also grateful to Colin Agur for his diligence and patience as copy editor.

Introduction
Crossing the Rubicon

On Thursday, 7 July 2005, in London, during the morning rush hour, coordinated terrorist attacks affected the public transportation network, shattered the morning routines of several million people, injured 770, and ended the lives of nearly five dozen. At 8:50 a.m., three bombs exploded in the tunnel between Kings Cross and Russell Square, and outside Edgware Road and Liverpool Street stations of the Underground. An hour later, another bomb exploded in a double decker bus at Tavistock Square, near Russell Square. These attacks were quickly dubbed "the London bombings," or "7/7."

Trapped in the London Underground, witnesses used their mobile phones to take pictures and make video recordings of the events as they unfolded. Unable to deploy journalists to the bombing sites, the BBC relied on eyewitness accounts and survivors' stories. Alexander Chadwick, a survivor, snapped a cellphone camera photograph of the evacuation of Kings Cross. Chadwick emailed the picture to yourpics@bbc.co.uk Around 11:30 a.m., the picture landed on the desks of BBC editors. It quickly became the iconic picture of the day. Other mainstream news media organisations such as *The New York Times* and The Times used that picture on their front pages in print and online. Chadwick's case was not isolated; as the day progressed, user-generated content became the main material journalists used to cover the attacks (Borenstein, 2009). In a speech in 2008, BBC News Director Helen Boaden recalled that:

> Within 24 hours, the BBC had received 1,000 stills and videos, 3,000 texts and 20,000 e-mails. What an incredible resource. Twenty-four hour television was sustained as never before by contributions from the audience; one piece on the Six O'clock News was produced entirely from pieces of user-generated content. At the BBC, we knew then that we had to change. We would need to review our ability to ingest this kind of material and our editorial policies to take account of these new forms of output.
>
> (Boaden, 2008)

Boaden also remembered that during these events, the BBC staff found that many of the amateur shots were "better than those supplied by the photographic agencies" (Boaden quoted in Barnes, 2008). The publication of Chadwick's picture on BBC News platforms was a watershed moment in BBC journalism. In the eyes of many journalists, including senior managers, the publication of that iconic picture highlighted the blurred boundaries and the new possibilities social networks created for journalists reporting crises.

The publication of Chadwick's picture also shed light on the tensions between journalists and audiences' accounts of events. Referring to the coverage of the London bombing attacks, Richard Sambrook, former Director at BBC Global News, said that, like never before, the audience became involved in telling stories to journalists:

> By day's end, the BBC's newsgathering had crossed a Rubicon. The quantity and quality of the public's contributions moved them beyond novelty, tokenism or the exceptional, and raises major implications that we are still working through. Not the least of these is how to handle this volume of material. Our small hub of four people was overwhelmed and is clearly going to be inadequate as we go forward. Of course, the BBC has used phone-ins, amateur video, and e-mail in its programs for years, but what was happening now was moving us way beyond where we'd been before.
>
> (Sambrook, 2005)

The BBC reacted to the influx of citizen material during 7/7 by building journalistic structures and processes to integrate this type of material into journalistic output. A User-Generated Content Hub journalist explains that a week after the bombings happened, the UGC Hub team was set up. 7/7

> Proved to be a hugely significant story from an audience content point of view–user-generated content point of view because the content that we were getting from the audience on that day was determining our agenda, for most of the stories. Because most news output reporting the official line, which was that there was a power stop in the underground. We saw pictures of a bus that had exploded at Tavistock Square.

7/7 was a significant news story for the BBC. Audiences helped a large, big-budget news organisation report the story with stark eyewitness pictures taken at the sites of the attacks. Audiences had quotes, details, and a chronology of events, allowing journalists to put the pieces of the puzzle together.

Before 7/7, audience material had shaped the news, from Abraham Zapruder's film of the Kennedy assassination in Dallas's Dealey Plaza to videos, pictures, and eyewitness accounts of the World Trade Center attacks on 11 September 2001 (Allan, 2013; Belair-Gagnon and Anderson,

2014; Borenstein, 2009). Each time, more and more people got a device, which became more useful for reporting. Today, the quantity, quality, and affordability of such devices (cameras and cell phones) make every citizen a potential reporter (Cornu, 2013). Today, the possibility of generating user-generated content exists for many more Zapruders than was the case in the early days of professional journalism in the late 1800s and 1900s (Gant, 2007).

On 7 July 2005, pictures, videos, and eyewitness accounts from the sites of the bombing attacks travelled through social media and e-mail, and landed on the BBC news desk. Journalists used this user-generated content material to put the story together. The journalistic uses of user-generated content continued for weeks after the attacks. On 21 July, a day of four attempted bombings, the BBC received 67 pictures and 33 videos, and a week later on the day of the arrest of the suspects, the BBC received an additional 20 pictures (Douglas, 2005). According to Richard Sambrook (2005), after 7/7, the BBC had crossed the Rubicon, signalling a turning point for the BBC's relationship with its audiences.

Although social media have allowed new forms of reporting and a stronger reliance on user-generated material in news production, BBC journalists continue to be concerned with how social media affect their daily work. Anchored in the ideals of public service, and with expectations that the broadcaster will pursue accuracy, balance, impartiality, and objectivity, the BBC faces a challenge: It seeks to incorporate social media into its reporting while maintaining its reputation and quality of content (Bennett, 2011). The BBC strives to maintain its authority with audiences (including licence fee payers),[1] and engage its audiences in a collaborative dialogue. This dynamic, involving social platforms-mediated communication between reporters and audiences, is at the core of this book.

This book explores the role of social platforms in crisis news production. It also uncovers social processes and tensions that have developed in professional practices and norms at the BBC. At its heart lies the idea that the BBC's struggle to understand and manage social media in its crisis reporting should be interpreted in the context of evolving journalistic conventions and the BBC in a period of politico-economic, cultural, socio-technological, and institutional change. The BBC's reimagination of social media is part of a large-scale project to become closer to its audiences. As Steve Barnett and Andrew Curry wrote, changes at the BBC "have not been achieved without conflict. Change is woven into British society and political life. [The BBC] has been praised and 'stripped open'" (Barnett and Curry, 1994,10).

CRISIS REPORTING IN A DIGITAL ERA

This book examines how journalists use social media, the ways in which social media have transformed BBC journalistic practices and relations with audiences, and how journalists and audiences articulate this new logic of communication in crisis reporting. Crisis reporting refers to "surprise events that challenge key organizational values and demand a swift response" (Olsson, 2010, 87). As a context for studying social media, crisis reporting is valuable for several reasons. In crises people's ordinary lives are interrupted, which prompts them to contribute user-generated content material to news organisations. And from the perspectives of the "people formerly known as audiences" and journalists, crisis reporting contributes to increased integration of social media in news.

Crisis reporting scholars have written that social media provide "a new space of reporting with significant consequences for what was covered, how and why" (Allan and Matheson, 2004, 7; Allan, 2013; Allan, Sonwalkar and Carter, 2007; Andersen, 2012; Balaji, 2011; Beckett, 2008; Chouliaraki, 2010; Riegert et al., 2010). The BBC has, for example, appropriated citizen journalism into its own "cosmopolitan vision" by incorporating "ordinary voices" in its news output, according to Lillie Chouliaraki (2010). This book explores the ways in which social media have led to transformations in journalistic norms and practices. It answers questions such as: Have social media enabled new spaces of reporting in which ordinary citizens contribute to traditional reporting? What kind of new structures within the newsroom have social media generated? And have social media allowed a more collaborative type of crisis reporting?

This book also extends the work of scholars such as Mervi Pantti, Karin Wahl-Jorgensen, and Simon Cottle to the case study of BBC News, crisis reporting, and social media. Journalists' reflections on their practice in crisis reporting shed light on how they perceive and perform witnessing. News work with respect to major disasters also highlights how journalists, correspondents, and news producers ground their "practices within the organisational and cultural milieu of contemporary news production" (Pantti et al., 2012, 93).

Placed in an international context, this book also explores the effects of social media on the largest public service broadcaster news production by examining news production processes and tensions in contexts of crisis reporting. It also answers the following questions: To what extent have social media transformed BBC journalistic practices and BBC relations with audiences? How have journalists reported crisis news events since 7/7 and what does this reportage tell us about journalistic practices and norms in crisis reporting? How have BBC journalistic structures changed in relation to social media, and what are the effects on power relations in the newsroom? By addressing these questions, I explore changing interactions between ordinary citizens witnessing and traditional journalists reporting global crisis news events.

Social media are global and have had a special significance in crisis reporting, such as coverage of the 2011 protests against authoritarian regimes in the Middle East and North Africa, commonly dubbed the "Arab Spring."

Journalists are also inclined to use social media in the context of crisis reporting, particularly where they cannot immediately access the area under scrutiny and must rely on sources in the field (Lotan et al., 2011, 1376). Moreover, social media are critical in domestic crisis reporting. For example, the Glasgow airport bombing in 2007 and crowdsourcing experiment with the London tube strike in 2010 each played a critical role in the BBC's adoption of social media. Other events, including the United Kingdom election in 2010, were important in terms of political candidates using Twitter. Although the BBC generally seeks to centralise its social media endeavors within the User-Generated Content Hub in London, BBC's four "nations",[2] such as BBC English regions, which include local television, radio, and web in England, the Isle of Man, and the Channel Islands, have developed their own social media goals and strategies. For instance, in 2011, BBC Cymru Wales hired two social media staff to manage social media activities in Wales. Journalists across the divisions of the BBC nevertheless remain accountable to the general rules binding the news organisation.

To explore social media at BBC News, this book gathered information from direct observation of the BBC newsroom, interviews with 50 journalists and senior managers, and document analysis of BBC reports, studies, and the websites of BBC News and the BBC Academy. Because I conducted my fieldwork in 2011, this book describes and analyses the usage of social media at the BBC especially from 2005 to 2011. This book also contextualises social media practices and norms within the history of the public broadcaster. Although since 2011 other global crises have occurred, including the conflict in Syria, this book focuses on the incorporation and usage of social media at the BBC, particularly until 2011.

Changes in journalism affect how journalists report crisis events. The sociological concept of "media logic" is useful to study changes in journalism (see Altheide and Snow, 1979; Dahlgren, 1996; Deuze, 2008). In crisis reporting, journalists use norms that are specific to their profession, including accuracy, impartiality, verification, and balance. These norms are, in turn, articulated in the new technological communication infrastructure (social media), which allows people to interact and leads to new power relations in the media logic and the news discourse presented to the audience. The media logic framework is helpful for understanding and conceptualising processes of management of social media in changing journalism norms, practices, and outputs.

BOOK STRUCTURE AND OVERVIEW OF CHAPTERS

This book explores the uses of social media in BBC crisis reporting since 7/7. In doing so, it looks at the norms and practices engendered by the socio-technological and politico-economic context in which journalists engage with social media. Chapter 1, "'Auntie' Takes on Social Media", traces the transformation of the BBC since the emergence of social media. This chapter describes how journalists have used social media in crisis reporting since 7/7 and how journalists have used a series of crisis events to reaffirm traditional journalistic norms and practices. I focus on the link between technologies and journalistic norms and practices in the context of the BBC. I argue that social media need to be understood in relation to sociopolitical changes occurring at the BBC and in crisis journalism. We should interpret the struggle to understand and manage social media in BBC journalism in the context of crisis reporting, journalistic conventions, and the BBC in a period of political, economic, cultural, and institutional shift. In Chapter 1, I show that the reimagination of social media in BBC journalism is part of a large-scale project of the BBC to become closer to its audiences.

Chapter 2, "Tweet or be Sacked!", provides an analysis of crisis reporting events between 2006 and 2010. I explore several significant crisis news events: the Saffron Revolution in Myanmar (2006), the Mumbai attacks (2008), the Iranian elections (2009), and the Haiti earthquake (2010). During these years, there is an increasing overlap for social media and journalism.

Chapter 3, "A New Order", discusses how, since post-2011, journalists recognize social media as part of their toolkit to improve their reporting. I argue that we should interpret the BBC's fight to understand and manage social media in the context of a period of political, economic, cultural, and institutional shifts.

Chapter 4, "New Structures, New Actors in the Newsrooms", maps and analyses the role played by tech-savvy journalists in articulating journalism in social media contexts, focusing on newsgathering. This chapter compares and contrasts changes in the structure of the newsroom over time. We notice the emergence of new structures within the newsroom and the new generation of tech-savvy journalists defining social media in BBC journalism. This is a breed of journalists that drove the BBC's early success online in the late 1990s. This chapter reflects on techies and the politico-economic, institutional, and socio-technological conditions that have led to the emergence of a new generation in the newsroom. In sum, the new generation of techies in the newsroom and the combined effects of politico-economic, social, institutional, and technological shifts suggest that journalism in crisis reporting has become much more collaborative.

The last chapter, "The Connected Newsroom", reflects on the extent to which social media have transformed BBC journalistic practices and relations with audiences, and how these transformations speak to broader issues of journalism, media institutions, and technologies. In this chapter, I shift my attention to the new media logic and outline the BBC's efforts to manage social media in its journalism. I also look at the emergence of new structures and actors in newsrooms. This chapter argues that journalists use values and practices that are specific to their profession, such as accuracy, impartiality, verification, and balance. These are, in turn, articulated in social media, which allow people to interact and give rise to new power relations in the media logic and the news discourse. I argue that whereas the BBC initially struggled to manage social media in its journalism, such have contributed to the architecture of information. This series of changes has led to a more collaborative approach to crisis reporting, insofar as new structures accommodating this new logic have supplanted the structures that existed in the media logic predating social media.

NOTES

1. The BBC licence fee model of financing involves the licence fee, a mandatory tax paid by all households who watch or record television in the UK. The colour licence is £145.50 (since 1 April 2009) and the black and white licence is £49 per household. Per month, the fees for a colour licence are divided as follow: £7.96 for TV, £2.11 for radio, £0.66 for online, and £1.40 for other costs such as investment in new technologies, running costs, digital, and collecting the licence fee. In 2010, the UK government froze the licence fees for the duration of the current BBC Charter period (through 2014). In the UK, during 2009–2010, 24,963,799 licences were in force. The licence fee pays for the television channels (BBC One, BBC Two, BBC Three, BBC Four, BBC News, BBC Parliament, CBBC, and CBeebies), radio services, digital radio services (BBC Radio 5 Live Sports Extra, BBC Radio 1Xtra, BBC Radio 7, BBC 6 Music, BBC Asian Network, regional television programmes, local radio services in England, national radio and television in Scotland, Wales, and Northern Ireland), BBC Red Button (BBC Connected Red, bringing online, TV, and radio content on one television, and BBC Red Button, an interactive service for digital television), BBC Mobile, and the BBC website. Households who watch broadcasting, whether it is on television, television on computers, mobile phones, or DVD, and video are required to pay the licence fee, but not every household with a television is forced to pay the fee. For example, anyone who is aged 74 years and older does not need to pay for a TV licence. There are other, more specific discounts: for example, legally blind people pay 50% of the fee (BBC, 2010d). In many instances, the BBC has been fighting for the survival of the licence fee model of financing. For example, the model faced a major test with the Thatcher government, which opposed the BBC's dedicated funding. In 1984, Prime Minister Thatcher suggested, "Why don't you take a little advertising? A minute or two on the hour or whatever" (cited in Barnett and Curry, 1994, 27). Thatcher made this comment in a context in which civil officials, journalists, and consumers discussed increasing the fee from £45 to £65 per year. In 1985, appalled by the potential rise of the licence fees, Thatcher appointed Sir Alan Peacock to lead a committee on the future of broadcasting with the intent of commercialising the BBC. This initiative was partly successful: the Peacock Committee on financing the BBC endorsed the licence fees by indexing them to the Retail Prices Index (RPI), as opposed to using taxation, sponsorship, or advertising models (Peacock Committee, 1986). Although the Peacock Committee on the financing of the BBC supported the licence fee model, the Committee enabled existence of the licence fee model within the framework of the RPI. Since the UK government policy initiatives of the 1980s and 1990s, the slow delegitimisation of the licence fee

model in the Peacock Committee (1986) and the Davies Committee (1999), the BBC has considered the licence fee as a protector of independence from political and commercial interests. The relationship involving consumers, the government (through the Royal Charter's renewal), the licence fee, and independence is an essential component of BBC's public broadcasting. According to the BBC, the licence fee model allows the organisation to freely experiment, talk about issues that journalists think are of public interest, and take risks that other news media will avoid because of the commercial risks involved (Simpson, 2002). The licence fee model provides a financial foundation for the BBC. The model also offers ideological independence from the government of the day, as shown by the BBC's ability to withstand the pro-advertising pressure brought by Thatcher's government. With a reliable financial foundation, the BBC states that it has been able to emphasise quality journalism.

2. BBC's four "nations" include BBC Scotland, BBC Wales, BBC Northern Ireland, and BBC English regions.

1 "Auntie" Takes On Social Media

The tweeting of the 'death' of congresswoman Gabrielle Giffords has provoked considerable and understandable debate about how mainstream media use Twitter. Those erroneous reports—on Twitter and elsewhere—raise important questions about how to correct information and whether to apologise and explain, as NPR does here. Should incorrect tweets be deleted? It's a question that crosses over to core editorial issues, like fact checking and sourcing. This debate is just the latest of several which, together, chart Twitter's inexorable evolution from a channel for casual conversation to a mainstream media platform.

(Matthew Eltringham, 2011)

THE EMERGENCE OF SOCIAL MEDIA AT BBC NEWS[1]

On 27 October 2004, Richard Sambrook, then BBC Director of Global News, spoke in New York at Columbia University's Graduate School of Journalism. In a talk entitled "Holding on to Objectivity", Sambrook suggested ways to promote objectivity in journalism in the 21st century.[2] He found that managing relationships with audiences is an essential part of the news organisation's service to the public. Thinking about the relationship between audience relations and technologies was nothing new at the time. In the early 2000s, Bill Kovach and Tom Rosenstiel's book, *The Elements of Journalism: What Newspeople Should Know and What the People Should Expect*,[3] and Dan Gilmor's book, *We the Media: Grassroots Journalism By the People, For the People*, were widely discussed internally at the BBC.

In his October 2004 speech, Sambrook pointed to the BBC's launch of News Watch on the BBC 24-hour news channel, where viewers could discuss BBC news coverage. The BBC had also launched a new website, also called News Watch, to explain editorial processes and policies to audiences. In his speech, Sambrook distinguished bloggers from journalists. He said that bloggers provide an extra source of information to journalists, but that they do not pretend to embody the principle of objectivity that is essential for BBC journalists. He added that the BBC possesses the resources to test, filter, and validate information. This speech reveals a change in the BBC's culture of journalism, with journalists' new, open attitude toward emerging media. Sambrook added that bloggers contribute to mainstream journalism by providing content and by examining content produced by others. He declared that new media would be integrated into BBC journalism, insofar as BBC journalists practiced transparency, remained independent, and followed an evidence-based journalism. Sambrook's speech raises a question: What are the institutional, politico-economic, socio-technological, and cultural transformations at the BBC that set the stage for changes in BBC journalism since 7/7? This chapter explores this social dynamic by discussing how journalists have used social media at the BBC in global crisis reporting.[4]

To have a better understanding of the BBC transformation, the current chapter reviews how journalists have used social media in crisis reporting since 7/7 and how journalists have used crisis events to reaffirm traditional journalistic norms and practices. I focus on the link between the materiality of technologies and the transformations of journalistic norms and practices in the context of the BBC. I argue that the impact of social media on journalism needs to be understood in relation to political changes occurring at the BBC and the industry. This chapter studies the BBC's struggle to understand and manage social media from the perspective of crisis reporting, journalistic conventions, and the BBC in a period of political, economic, cultural, and institutional shift. The BBC's reimagination of social media is part of a large-scale BBC project to become closer to its audiences.

THE BBC AND AUDIENCE PARTICIPATION

Audience involvement in journalism has a history that predates the emergence of social media. Audience material contributed to news coverage long before the emergence of online news and social media. The popular radical press in England in the late 18th century and mid-19th century comprised elements of citizen journalism partly because of its activist stances and audience contribution to reportages (Curran and Seaton, 2003). In the 1740s, American citizens distributed political pamphlets in New York, Philadelphia, and Boston. The practice of these pamphleteers was elevated in 1776 by Thomas Paine's *Common Sense*, of which approximately 150,000 copies were printed and distributed. On both sides of the Atlantic, pamphleteers demonstrated that audiences could play an active role in news production (Schudson, 2003, 73). In the 1920s, free radio stations, or pirate radio, involved community activists who broadcasted offshore in parts of Europe and the UK. On 22 November 1963, Abraham Zapruder documented the assassination of U.S. President John F. Kennedy using his Bell & Howell camera; he later sold the print and film rights for $200,000 to Life Magazine

(Allan, 2013, 68; Belair-Gagnon and Anderson, 2014; Boaden, 2008; Woodward, 2003). On 3 March 1991, from the balcony of his apartment, George Holliday filmed Rodney King being beaten by Los Angeles Police Department officers, creating a recording using his Sony Handycam. The pricing and popularity of these devices prompted the creation of television programmes such as America's Funniest Home Videos. Following these events, new digital platforms in this emergent communication field transformed journalism practices and norms (Allan, 2007).[5] For instance, the BBC took initiatives to involve the community in its reporting before the emergence of social media in its journalism (Sambrook, 2005).

The BBC has been a player in online journalism since the early 1990s. In 2001, *Digital Storytelling* was a flagship project taking digital media production tools into communities in the United Kingdom. Since digital storytelling projects started, the BBC has trained hundreds of citizens across the country to shoot and edit their multimedia packages for broadcast in BBC outputs (Wardle and Williams, 2008). People told their stories and learned the craft of journalism, and people's stories were produced in short programmes and broadcasted on BBC News or other programmes (Sambrook, 2005). In 2003, Argyll and Bute Council on the West Coast of Scotland started *Digital Communities*, a Scottish Executive project. Every household in the North Argyll Islands received a personal computer and a narrowband web connection. BBC Scotland launched Island Blogging with the community of the island. In November 2003, the BBC's Action Network launched a website to help citizens become more involved in their community. Citizens exchanged concerns and organised campaigns on the website. In addition, the BBC provided guides on how to negotiate civic life, briefings, and a database of organisations (Sambrook, 2005).

Audience participation has been part of the BBC since its creation. Yet BBC journalists trace the emergence of social media to the increase in accumulation of audience material and user-generated content, as well as journalistic and citizens' uses of this material in reporting events. Journalists also associate the emergence of social media with an institutional response to the availability of these media following the Asian tsunami in 2004 (Eltringham, 2010).[6] At that time, the main sources of citizen material were e-mail and mobile phones: Citizens took pictures on their mobile phones and used the e-mail function on these devices to send photos to the BBC.[7] This confluence of technologies (camera and e-mail) turned a trickle of citizen material into a torrent.

THE 2004 ASIAN TSUNAMI: THE RISE
OF UGC IN JOURNALISM

On Boxing Day 2004, a powerful earthquake (9.3 on the Richter scale) in the Indian Ocean created a tsunami that affected several countries. What is referred to as the South Asian Tsunami, the 2004 Indian Ocean Tsunami, or the Boxing Day Tsunami devastated parts of Indonesia, Thailand, and Sri Lanka; it also caused damage as far away as East Africa. The countries that suffered casualties and damages included Australia, Bangladesh, India, Indonesia, Kenya, Madagascar, Malaysia, Mauritius, Myanmar, Oman, L'île de la Réunion, Seychelles, Singapore, Somalia, South Africa, Sri Lanka, Thailand, Tanzania, the Maldives, and Yemen. In the hours and days that followed, the BBC received thousands of unsolicited videos, mobile phone pictures, and eyewitness accounts of the events from individuals in affected areas.

The tsunami marks the emergence of social media (recognised as audience material and user-generated content at the time) in BBC journalism. During this event, the accumulation of user-generated content in traditional journalism increased exponentially and the line between audience and journalism became less distinct. The confluence of new technologies and the ability of the audience and the news organisation to create new meanings around news production triggered these drastic changes in journalism. Individuals in places affected by the tsunami initially did not realise the scale of the event; meanwhile, because of user-generated content sent in from affected areas, faraway audiences in distant places knew that the tsunami had hit many countries in the Indian Ocean. For example, information on the tsunami in Sri Lanka reached Western media outlets before any news reached the population settled in Banda Aceh, Indonesia. Phone calls from ordinary citizens who witnessed the events reached the Agence France Presse (AFP) and Lanka Business Online journalists. Lanka Business Online broke the story online at 3:34 a.m. and the AFP sent the news agency dispatch at 3:46 a.m. UTC (Samarajiva, 2005, 734–735). Other major news organisations faced similar challenges.

The Asian tsunami was a turning point for crisis reporting (Gilmor, 2005; Allan and Thorsen, 2010). Thomas H. Glocer, at the time the Chief Executive Officer of Thomson Reuters, said that on the day of the main event, none of Reuters's 2,300 journalists or 1,000 stringers were at the site of the events: "For the first 24 hours", he said, "the best and only photographs came from tourists armed with telephones, digital cameras and camcorders. If you didn't have those pictures, you weren't on the story" (Glocer quoted in Cooper, 2011, 6). In other words, stories were becoming more focused on people's lives as newsrooms opened up their doors (Beckett, 2008).[8]

During the news coverage of the events, citizens contributed to journalism with firsthand reports (Allan et al., 2007, 376). This material was mainly sent via e-mail and mobile phones to relatives and then sent to news organisations. Technorati.com, a blog-monitoring tool, registered about 55,000 tsunami-related blogs on the first three days following the events. 10,000 more blogs followed (Allan et al., 2007). At the time, Facebook was restricted to university students and Twitter did not yet exist. Witnesses sent in material to the BBC by peer-to-peer methods, especially e-mail, and via the BBC website message board. Kevin Bakhurst, former Controller of BBC News Channel, said:

> The power of the Internet and email was demonstrated for the first time [with the tsunami] . . . The BBC website suddenly became a major source of information where people were trying to find out about friends and relatives. It became a public service in that way, but also just in terms of us getting in contact with people telling their stories . . . it became a real source as well.
>
> (Bakhurst cited in Cooper, 2011, 18)

The BBC had received thousands of eyewitness accounts from audience members telling their stories about the tsunami. By the end of the first week following the tsunami, BBC News Online had received about 50,000 e-mails. Hannah Howard, BBC's spokesperson, divided e-mails into four main categories: "People from the UK trying to get information on friends and family in South East Asia; people in Asia e-mailing in to say they were safe; people sharing their stories and experiences; and appeals for help" (Allan et al., 2007, 378). The BBC website message board recorded approximately 400,000 visitors during that same time period (Allan et al., 2007, 378). Many people wrote comments on the BBC website message board and, as a result, some were able to be reunited with their friends and loved ones. For example, an audience member with the online username Pip wrote, "Our thanks to the BBC for getting us news of Harish Sankaran. He's alive and well and back with us" (BBC, 2005b).

At the time of the tsunami, digital technologies—including the Internet, specifically e-mail and blogs, digital cameras, and camera phones—had evolved insofar as audiences at the scene of the events were able to share in real time eyewitness accounts with professional journalists. At the same time, the availability of social media and the ability of audiences to contribute to news production transformed the journalistic content and technique. Journalists were getting closer geographically and subject-wise to the communities that they were talking to (Beckett, 2008). In that sense, the South Asian tsunami marked a transformative moment in BBC crisis reporting. At the BBC, audiences contributed more to news production of crisis events, although not as journalists' equals. On the BBC website, editors allocated specific spaces for citizens who had witnessed the event and sent in video and pictures. The tsunami created a precedent in BBC journalism. From the perspective of the BBC, the tsunami signalled the need to manage this kind of material.

Following the tsunami, in March 2005, Director General of BBC Mark Thompson spoke to BBC staff about the Corporation's transformations. Thompson said, "we plan £32 million of new money to help New Media develop platforms and navigation to support not just existing digital streams but news on demand and two-way applications: new ways for the public to enjoy, interact with and contribute to BBC content" (Thompson, 2005). The BBC General Manager's speech emphasised that senior managers were planning to invest in new media platforms following a trend dating back to the 1990s. In the 1990s, the BBC was becoming a major international player and vanguard of new technologies, such as through its partnership with the publisher Pearson (Barnett and Curry, 1994, 222). Thompson's speech also suggested that the BBC would make user-generated content a key part of this development. The BBC UGC Hub thus has origins that predate 7/7; it is part of a larger institutional effort to push the public broadcaster to be leader in new media in the United Kingdom.

THE LONDON BOMBING ATTACKS

At the BBC, on 7 July 2005, another breaking news story confirmed the growing significance of user-generated content in BBC journalism: the London bombing attacks. Ordinary citizens' eyewitness accounts had already proven significant for global audiences, such as during the 11 September 2001 terrorists attacks (Allan 2013; Andén-Papadopoulos, 2013, 2). The key challenge for the BBC during these events was to make sense of citizen engagement in BBC traditional journalism.

In July 2005, half a year into the user-generated content pilot project, social media played a more critical role in the coverage of a disaster much closer to home than the Asian tsunami. In early July 2005, several BBC journalists, including Vicky Taylor and Matthew Eltringham, were sitting in the BBC News website newsroom discussing what to do with audience material and managing a user-generated content pilot project not yet institutionalised as the "UGC Hub".[9] That team was part of the News Interactive section of the newsroom, located five floors above the multimedia newsroom in the Television Centre in White City, West London.

At the time, the proposition to set up a UGC Hub had "met with some scepticism from senior quarters in BBC News and very nearly did not happen" (Eltringham, 2010). The BBC was not sure how it would affect its journalism or ideals, including accuracy, impartiality, and objectivity[10] (Douglas, 2006). Only a handful of journalists at the BBC used social media, most of them early technological adopters, including editors writing on the BBC's "The Editors" blog.

On 7 July 2005, BBC senior managers saw the idea of a UGC Hub in a new light: During the London bombing attacks, the small BBC News Interactive team, located on the 7th floor of the BBC Television Centre, played a critical role in managing user-generated content. As in the case of the Asian tsunami, the events of 7/7 showed the increasing importance of social media in BBC journalism.

"News that morning had punctured the euphoria surrounding the city's Olympic success, the decision to award the Games having been announced the previous day", wrote media scholar Stuart Allan (2007, 4). When the first bombings occurred, there were no journalists at the sites of the attacks. That day, the UGC Hub team allowed the BBC to follow the events as they unfolded. " 'In 56 minutes,' an Associated Press (AP) reporter observed, 'a city fresh from a night of Olympic celebrations was enveloped in eerie, blood-soaked quiet' " (Allan, 2007, 4). From their desks, journalists relied on all types of sources to cover the story, from eyewitness accounts to pictures taken at the bombing sites:

> For many Londoners, especially those who were deskbound in their workplaces, the principal source of breaking news about the attacks was the Internet. In contrast with the mobile telephone companies, Internet service providers were largely unaffected by the blasts although several news websites came under intense pressure from the volume of traffic directed to them (overall, traffic to news websites was up nearly 50 per cent from the previous day, according to online measurement companies.
>
> (Allan, 2007, 5)

Audiences located at the site of the tragic events were able to share eyewitness accounts, and journalists put them to use in their stories. "Within minutes our email inbox was out of control. It was clear that something was happening, but we had no idea how to manage the huge number of emails we were receiving and the information they were giving us", wrote Matthew Eltringham (2010).

Eltringham remembers that late in the morning, a picture arrived in one e-mail. That picture, of passengers walking down a London underground tunnel towards the light, was taken by Alexander Chadwick and became the iconic image of the day. Chadwick e-mailed the picture to yourpics@bbc. co.uk Around 11:30 a.m., the picture landed on the desks of BBC editors. It was the second picture that the BBC had received that day, but it was the first shot from the underground. Eltringham then

> Spoke to an output editor on the News Channel (or News 24 as it was then) who was initially reluctant to run it. She, I think, said they already had a picture and didn't need another one—meaning the scarf one. After an extended conversation—reinforced by a couple of others from various colleagues they eventually ran it around about lunchtime. Once they'd seen it, and all of Tavistock Square pictures started coming in, they ran it intensively throughout the afternoon and evening.[11]

Alexander Chadwick's picture, sent by e-mail to the BBC, was a significant symbolic moment for BBC uses of user-generated material; BBC journalists used user-generated content as the main source of information to cover the 7/7 bombings. In the hours and days that followed, user-generated content came in large quantities and, in certain cases such as Chadwick's photo, in high journalistic quality. Journalists at other news organisations, such as the Guardian Unlimited, also gathered information from their audiences to cover the news. By 10:15 a.m., the blog-tracking service Technorati collected approximately 1,300 posts from the blasts (Allan, 2007). At the BBC, journalists managed the story using Microsoft Outlook with the emerging UGC Hub team and the wider BBC News production staff. Matthew Eltringham recalls that the gathering of information "was all done by .jpeg and email. The output platform then turned it into an appropriate form that allowed them to broadcast and publish it".[12]

That the BBC Interactive team and user-generated content had played a central role in managing incoming material during 7/7 demonstrated the significance of the emergence of social media in BBC journalism. The demand to manage user-generated content material led to the rise of a new generation of tech-savvy journalists in the newsroom. Helen Boaden, BBC News Director, said that during 7/7, the scope and reach of user-generated content was greater than before. She stated that within 24 hours, the Corporation received more than 1,000 pictures and videos, 3,000 text messages, and 20,000 e-mails (Boaden, 2008). The amount of user-generated content in news stories was unprecedented: "Twenty-four hour television was sustained as never before by contributions from the audience; one piece on the Six O'clock News was produced entirely from pieces of user-generated content" (Boaden, 2008). Torin Douglas, BBC News Media correspondent, confirmed that "dramatic stills and video sequences from passengers on the Tube trains led the BBC Six O'clock News . . . They not only conveyed the choking, claustrophobic atmosphere but also provided significant evidence, helping identify the time of the explosions" (Douglas, 2006). Reflecting on 7/7, Richard Sambrook added that ordinary citizen eyewitnesses had become part of BBC storytelling during these events. The Interactive news team filtered this storytelling (Sambrook, 2005). BBC News Online pointed to the volume of images and clips that the website received during the events:

> About 70 images and five clips were used on the BBC's website and in television newscasts. 'London explosions: Your photos' presented still images, while one example of a video clip was an 18-second sequence of a passenger evacuating an underground station, taken with a camera phone video. 'It certainly showed the power of what our users can do, Clifton added, when they are close to a terrible event like this'.
> (BBC News Online, 8 July 2005 in Allan, 2007)

The London bombing attacks were a watershed moment for user-generated content. The practice of user-generated content was not new at the broadcaster; before the bombings, London BBC News Interactive received on average 300 e-mails a day (Wardle and Williams, 2010, 781). The volume of user-generated content received by the Corporation was unprecedented.

7/7 was "a very significant story where social media platforms helped journalists reporting the story" and the BBC realised the potential of the user-generated content pilot project and the increasingly significant role of tech-savvy journalists in the multimedia newsroom.[13]

In addition to managing social media through the UGC Hub, news organisations including the BBC "created spaces for first-hand accounts from eyewitnesses to the attacks" (Allan, 2007, 6). The BBC's "Reporters' Log: London Explosions" allowed ordinary citizens to share eyewitness accounts of the events (Allan, 2007, 146). The first log reads:

> Jon Brain: Edgware Road: 1115 BST
> There's been a scene of chaos and confusion all morning here but it's beginning to settle down. The entire area around the tube station has been sealed off and there are dozens of emergency vehicles here.
> We've seen a number of walking wounded emerge from the station, many of them covered with blood and obviously quite distraught. They are being treated at a hotel opposite the tube station.
> The concern now is whether there are still people trapped inside the tube station underground. I've seen a team of paramedics go into the station in the last half hour.
>
> (quoted in Allan, 2007, 146)

The BBC allowed audience members to post on the page "London explosions: your accounts". That page asked, "Did you witness the terrorist attacks in London? How have the explosions affected you"? This BBC webpage allowed audiences to send in experiences and photos to the BBC. The BBC editors read the posts before publishing them on the website. Blogs and other social media were also important in reporting the attacks. For example, citizens posted a number of photos on Moblog. co.uk, a British website allowing people to take pictures and videos with a camera phone and publish them on the Internet. An image taken by Adam Stacey was viewed more than 36,000 times on the website by the early evening (Allan, 2007, 146). Flickr.com received about 300 photos in the eight hours following the attacks (Allan, 2007, 146). "There appears to be little doubt—in the eyes of both advocates and critics alike—that citizen reporting is having a profound impact on the forms, practices and epistemologies of mainstream journalism" (Allan, 2007, 146). At the BBC, the rise of user-generated content management called attention to the central newsgathering role that a user-generated content hub started taking on within the news organisation.[14]

Following 7/7, and with the support of senior managers who realised the significance of user-generated content, the small team in the BBC News Interactive service that set up a pilot project to manage social media became the UGC Hub. The objective of this project was to find out the news value of audiences' ability to use new technologies such as mobile phones, and send news organisations images or videos of breaking news (Eltringham, 2010).[15] Following 7/7, the BBC formally created the UGC Hub to collect and manage incoming material.[16] Created post-7/7 2005, the UGC Hub was initially led by Vicky Taylor, Editor of Interactivity at the BBC, and Matthew Eltringham. Taylor and Eltringham were both part of BBC Interactive, located on the 7th floor of the BBC White City, London building. Journalists have used user-generated content in the past, but it was not subject to systematic review by a major news organisation. This change in the newsroom is not unique to the BBC. In 2013, *The New York Times* added three editors to its social media desk. The team strives to integrate readers in its journalism, particularly in moment-to-moment updates in crisis reporting such as in the Boston Marathon bombings (Roston et al., 2013). For a UGC Hub journalist, the UGC Hub acted as the central clearinghouse for social media gathering. "At the same time we just shared it on email with the News website".[17]

The UGC Hub originally had two main objectives. The first was to collect user-generated content such as videos, pictures, eyewitness accounts, and story leads. The second objective was to monitor BBC website discussions. In that context, the growing volume and role of user-generated content confirmed the need for a hub coming from that team. Early in the emergence of social platforms online, it was the centralised user-generated content team of tech-savvy journalists who took the lead in integrating social media in journalism. The UGC Hub became the unit responsible for managing social media intakes.

Although the Hub's centralised newsgathering structure suggests a centralisation of social media management in the hands of techies (tech-savvy journalists), due to the structure of the news organisation, other BBC newsrooms continued to receive user-generated content independently of the UGC Hub. The creation of the UGC Hub post-7/7 thus "signalled that central BBC decision-makers were taking 'audience content' and 'audience comment' seriously" (Wardle and Williams, 2010, 795). And the importance BBC executives gave to user-generated content was emulated in a 2008 speech Boaden delivered at e-Democracy. She declared that the BBC knew that it had to change and review its ability to manage new media in its editorial policies (Boaden, 2008).

The story of social media during the BBC coverage of the 2005 London bombing attacks also demonstrates how audiences were able to contribute to news production via the Internet. The communicative power of citizens and traditional journalists is increasingly consolidated. As Daniel Bennett corroborates, "how the BBC negotiates these tensions in the future will continue to influence the way the corporation's journalism is produced in the 21st Century. But 'You' will certainly be having a big say" (Bennett, 2013). This partly explains why the pilot project was set up and supported by BBC senior management.[18]

THE BBC'S WHITE PAPER: A PUBLIC SERVICE FOR ALL

The 2006 White Paper, titled "A Public Service for All: The BBC in the Digital Age", highlighted the increasing importance of new information technologies, including social media, in BBC journalism (Department of Culture, Media and Sports, 2006). The paper was a statement of the government's policy based on two years of consultation, research, and public debate involving thousands of people including policy makers, audience members, and the BBC staff. These thousands of participants commented on the White Paper, which, in turn, was transformed into the new Royal Charter and the Agreement put in front of the Parliament in July 2006. "The Charter sets out the public purposes of the BBC, guarantees its independence,[19] and outlines the duties of the Trust and the Executive Board", and the Agreement sitting alongside the Charter "also covers the BBC's funding and its regulatory duties" (BBC, 2013). The Charter is renewed every 10 years. Since 2006 the BBC nevertheless made amendments to the agreement due to legal and structural changes in the media ecology. Some of those changes include the March 2010 amendment to reflect changes in United Kingdom laws due to the implementation of the Audio Visual Media Services directive and the 21 October 2010 licence fee settlement. The current Charter runs until 31 December 2016.

The 2006 White Paper redefined the BBC's purposes. These new purposes included playing a leading role in technological development and five essential characteristics for all BBC content: high quality, challenging, original, innovative, and engaging. The paper recommended relaunching the BBC's website, which had been initiated in 1994 (Curran and Seaton, 2003, 281). The paper suggested that the website should incorporate more personalisation, richer audio-visuals, and user-generated content. This process was facilitated partly by a shift toward the Internet Protocol television (IPTV), starting in the mid-1990s. IPTV allowed video on demand (VOD) or audio and video on demand (AVOD). VOD or AVOD is a non-linear rather than linear programming model, which means that Internet users can choose to select, listen, and/or watch video or audio material on demand, catch-up television, and live television online as opposed to watching or listening to video or audio material at a scheduled broadcast time.

Since the 2006 White Paper's recommendations, the BBC has put together a set of principles that have taken into account the increasing role of new information technologies in BBC journalism. These principles entail an organisational shift in energies and resources into continuous news on TV, radio, broadband, and mobile. The BBC promoted a new pan-platform journalism strategy, consisting of mobile devices, putting 24/7 news on the web, broadband, TV, and radio.

The BBC's new journalistic practices are a reflection of policies and "are historically situated conceptualisations of the public interest and 'public value'" (Klontzas, 2008). The 2006 White Paper defines public value as the value the United Kingdom licence fee payers put in the BBC service, the contribution the BBC delivers to society, and the value for money the service delivers to its public.

During this process, in April 2006, the BBC unveiled an editorial endeavour designed to deliver more value to its audiences: *Creative Future* (BBC, 2006; Jones and Salter, 2012, 82). This editorial endeavour reflected "the long-term commitment of the BBC to transform itself into a broadcaster for the digital age, spending at least £106 million a year [out of its £4 billion a year licence fee budget guaranteed now until 2012] on its new media 'find, play and share' strategy" (Klontzas, 2008). To position the BBC in the new media logic, the BBC deployed *Creative Future*'s strategy to "find, play and share" in five ways: (1) Keeping BBC "legacy products," such as the websites, as the core of informing, educating, and entertaining audiences; (2) Moving audio-visual to on demand so that the content is available anywhere, anytime via iPlayer (commonly called the "martini media" philosophy); (3) Sharing user-generated formats by means of "digital campfires" such as message boards; (4) Commissioning new formats on new media; (5) Acting as a guide to the Internet and providing easy access to audiences across the United Kingdom across digital platforms such as mobile phones and the Internet (BBC, 2006; Klontzas, 2008). The "technophilia" of the BBC is not new; the Corporation has demonstrated historically that technological innovation is important to its journalistic mandate. "[T]he White Paper's proposals . . . go beyond a simple acknowledgement of the BBC's role in stimulating digital take-up to include a heavily prescriptive demand that it leads audiences into a digital future" (Freedman, 2008, 52).

The BBC displayed their strategy toward new media in the 10-year (2006–2016) BBC Royal Charter, which stated that the BBC would be "promoting its other purposes, helping to deliver to the public the benefits of emerging communications technologies and services and, in addition, taking a leading role in the switchover to digital television" (Department of Culture, Media and Sports, 2006b, §4). The BBC's vision toward emerging new information technologies was contextualised in the Royal Charter. Shortly after the unveiling of *Creative Future*, in 2008 the BBC announced that it would undergo institutional changes to make the web and the user-generated content in the middle of the journalistic operation (Horrocks, 2008). "This Internet-led 'self-styled' reinvention was intended to fundamentally change the way the BBC interacted with its new digital audiences" (Jones and Salter, 2012, 82).

TAKING SOCIAL NETWORKING SERIOUSLY

The UGC Hub's creation is the upshot of several enabling conditions in the new media logic: the availability of new information technologies, including social media; the increasing role of tech-savvy journalists in BBC news production; the direction of United Kingdom government policy; the interests of senior managers and journalists; and preexisting organisational structures, journalistic norms, and practices. In other words, technologies of news production are socially and culturally shaped.[20] More than a mere structural feature of BBC News, the UGC Hub represented a new form of experimentation with audiences and social media, and an attempt by the BBC to make sense of new information technologies. In this context, 7/7 was a watershed moment signifying the emergence of social media within the BBC's UGC Hub.

NOTES

1. A version of this chapter is published in: Belair-Gagnon, V. (2012) 'Technology, Cultural Policy and the Public Service Broadcasting Tradition: Professional Practices at the BBC News in the Social Media Turn', pp. 112–131 in J. Paquette (ed.), *Cultural Policy, Work and Identity: The Creation, Renewal and Negotiation of Professional Subjectivities*. Farnham: Ashgate.
2. Sambrook spoke after the Hutton Report. The Report criticised the reporting of a BBC journalist, Andrew Gillian, which made allegations that the British government of Tony Blair knew that it was wrong that Saddam Hussein could launch attacks of weapons of mass destruction with 45 minutes when claims were made in the government's intelligence dossier on Iraq, and which subsequently led to a leak of a source, Dr. Kelly, who eventually committed suicide.
3. In *The Elements of Journalism: What Newspeople Should Know and the Public Should Expect*, Bill Kovach and Tom Rosenstiel discuss nine essential elements of journalism fulfilling a democratic function in society: (1) journalism's first obligation is the truth, (2) journalism's first loyalty is citizens, (3) the essence of journalistic discipline is verification, (4) practitioners must maintain independence from those that they cover, (5) journalism must serve as an independent monitor of power, (6) journalism must provide a forum for public criticism and compromise, (7) journalism must strive to make what is significant interesting and relevant, (8) journalism must keep the news comprehensive and proportional, and (9) its practitioners must be allowed to exercise their personal conscience.
4. Journalists' social media uses are contextual. A journalist might not use social media in Afghanistan because the nature of reporting is more based on personal networks or reporting embedded in the U.S. army bases. New information technologies have an impact on journalism that is undeniable and it has been shown through news stories since 2004. For this reason, it is worth taking a look at this. Christina Archetti published an article on the changing practices of foreign correspondents in London. She wrote, "the results confirm that foreign correspondence is indeed changing, but that its reality is far more nuanced and variegated than current literature would lead to understand. The analysis of the correspondents' practice suggests that the alleged 'crisis' of journalism might affect some countries more than others, certain media (like newspapers) more than other kinds of outlets (magazines, for instance). Overall, rather than necessarily leading to 'churnalism'—or the trend to endlessly recycle secondhand unchecked material—the development of global media can also support deeper and higher-quality reporting" (Archetti, 2013).

5. A more complete descriptive analysis and conceptualisation of citizen media can be found in: Belair-Gagnon, V., & Anderson, C. W. (2014) 'Citizen Media and Journalism', in R. Mansell & P. Ang (eds.), *The International Encyclopedia of Digital Communication*, New York: Blackwell-Wiley and International Communication Association (ICA).

6. UGC Hub journalist, interview 2011.

7. UGC Hub journalist, interview 2011.

8. Danny Schechter, media critic, stated that the tsunami media coverage was an example of "helicopter journalism": In his view, it is "like the foreign correspondent who flies into a conflict zone for an afternoon and gets most of his information from a taxi driver". The limits of such forms of "parachute" reporting are readily apparent, he argues, when one considers how distanced it is from what is actually happening on the ground away from the rescue helicopters. In this sense, the item in question may be considered broadly indicative of much Western news reporting of the tsunami's aftermath (Schechter quoted in Allan et al., 2007, 375).

9. UGC Hub journalist, interview 2011.

10. Senior Manager World News, interview 2011.

11. UGC Hub journalist, e-mail exchange 19 March 2012.

12. UGC Hub journalist, e-mail exchange 19 March 2012.

13. Assistant Editor Social Media, interview 2011.

14. Note that the centralisation of the news followed the 1990s broadcasting models of News and Current Affairs, in which John Birt, former Director General of the BBC from 1992 to 2000, centralised radio and television newsgathering operations within a single Newsgathering department. This department served reports to radio and television outlets. In 1996, the World Service international newsgathering arm folded into the domestic department, leading towards more packaged news (Born, 2004, 389).

15. World News Senior Manager, interview 2011.

16. UGC Hub journalist, interview 2011.

17. UGC Hub journalist, e-mail exchange 19 March 2012.

18. Before the London bombings, social media engagement was present in the BBC's managerial discourse and actions.

19. Political and financial independence developed in the early broadcasting days of the BBC. The Sykes Committee in 1923 and the Crawford Committee in 1925 provided background for BBC independence. The Sykes Committee recommended funding based on licence fees, no advertising, and that the broadcaster transfer from private to public. The report stated that wavebands in the country should have been regarded in British society as pieces of public property. The wavebands that would be assigned would be subject to "safeguards" to "protect public interests". The control of such power would remain in the hands of the state, rather than corporate interests. The Crawford Committee recommended that a public service corporation run broadcasting, licence fee funding for 10 years, education programmes, and no direct parliamentary control. On 14 July 1926, the UK Postmaster General recommended that the British government accept the recommendations of the Committee. After the Committee published its report, the BBC was created and derived its authority from the Royal Charter. From its institutional origins, the BBC was said to operate at arm's length from political and commercial interests. Although the Sykes and the Crawford Committees defined the BBC as independent from political and commercial interests, the General Strike in 1926 placed the Corporation in a conflicting position by testing the BBC's principles of impartiality and independence (Curran and Seaton, 2003, 114). By raising public concerns about BBC editorial independence, the strike was an important

steppingstone in confirming the importance of the BBC as a national public broadcaster free from political and financial influence (Williams, 2010, 100). "Reith knew that the survival of the Corporation [whose constitution had not yet been formally accepted] depended on its conduct during the crisis" and took actions favouring the government (Williams, 2010, 115). The Hankey Television Committee (commissioned on September 1943 and reported 29 December 1944) recommended that television should retain its financial independence and that the BBC keep its monopoly until 1956. The Beveridge Report (commissioned on 21 June 1949 and reported 15 December 1950) recommended the maintenance of licence fees. One of the Beveridge Committee's members, Selwyn Lloyd, MP, opposed the Report and was in favour of the end of the BBC's monopoly. This paved the way toward the creation of a second British broadcaster. Once the Conservatives returned to power in 1950, recommendations that resembled those of Selwyn Lloyd were drafted in a White Paper and ITV was created in 1954. The Pilkington Committee (commissioned on 13 July 1960 and reported 27 June 1962) endorsed the renewal of the BBC Charter and the continued funding of the BBC through licence fees. The Annan Report (commissioned on 10 April 1974 and reported 24 February 1977) resulted in the increase of the licence fees. The Report also led to the creation of a fourth independent television channel, Channel 4, and its Welsh counterpart, Sianel Pedwar Cymru, in 1982 under the leadership of the conservative government of Margaret Thatcher, following BBC1, BBC2, and ITV. BBC independence was central in the Annan Report. The Report expressed the importance of BBC's independence through the continuation of the licence fee model (Annan, 1977). But the licence fee is a double-edged sword; in times of controversy, the BBC is dependent on licence fee payers, who could be critical of its actions. Whereas the licence fee system gives the BBC day-to-day independence, BBC executives know that every 10 years they must renegotiate that agreement. The BBC has independence, but it is an independence based on trust and respect. If the BBC loses the trust of the government or a critical mass of licence holders, it could be severely weakened. The independence of the BBC is thus conditional, not absolute. In 1985, Thatcher appointed Alan Peacock, a liberal political economist and specialist in fiscal and welfare economics, as chairperson of the inquiry on the future of broadcasting in the United Kingdom (Potschka, 2012). The Peacock Committee (commissioned on 27 March 1985) issued its report on 29 May 1986, and recommended indexing licence fees to the RPI. The Committee also supported the emergence of independent television production companies. In addition, the Committee said that voluntary subscriptions would be more equitable and efficient in answering consumers' needs (Peacock Committee, 1986). In 1999, the independent review panel, the Davies Committee (commissioned on 14 October 1998 and reported 28 July 1999), chaired by the economist Gavyn Davies, made the case for freezing licence fees from 2001 onward, BBC savings, and income coming only from BBC domestic services. At the same time the Committee firmly recommended against advertising, sponsorship, and subscription (Kaufman, 2004, 35). From the 1980s onward, the original meaning of the licence fee model of funding has been redefined. The BBC did not enjoy the same financial gains that it did at the early stages of public broadcasting, meant to guarantee independence from political and commercial interests. From the 1980s onwards we acknowledge a transition from a sociocultural broadcasting approach toward a free market vision of broadcasting policy (Born, 2005; Potschka, 2012).

20. See *Alexander, 2006*, as well as Cottle and Ashton, 1999 for more cultural research on news.

2   Tweet or Be Sacked!

Questions of truth, trust, bias, partisanship, and verification have been raised since the first steps in public communication. In today's environment of democratised mass digital media they are as important as ever. However, the ideas of impartiality and objectivity—at the heart of serious news journalism for most of the last century—are now under pressure and even attack in the digital age. They emerged as journalistic norms to describe a professional editorial discipline that sought to avoid personal and political biases and to encourage trust in newspaper journalism.

(Sambrook, 2012)

THE INTEGRATION OF SOCIAL MEDIA

Up to 2006, social media remained largely separate from the daily work routine of many BBC journalists. Only a handful of journalists and the UGC Hub team integrated social media into their daily journalistic work. Senior managers and tech-savvy journalists were taking social media seriously, even though social media were a nascent enterprise in BBC journalism. From 2006 to 2010, a series of watershed crisis news events allowed social media to be used systematically in BBC journalism. At the same time, the public broadcaster took more steps within the newsroom to combine social media in BBC journalism, and on new social media platforms such as Twitter. Between 2006 and 2010 the new media logic involved social media, citizens, and journalism. Several crisis news events of significance show that the broadcaster took more steps to integrate social media in BBC journalism: the Saffron Revolution in Myanmar of 2006, the Mumbai attacks of 2008, the Iranian elections of 2009, and the Haiti earthquake of 2010. As communication scholar Adrienne Russell wrote, "Networked publics are replacing passive consumers and, together with digital tools and news industry economics, changing the way journalism is produced, circulated, and discussed" (Russell, 2010, 98).

THE SAFFRON REVOLUTION IN MYANMAR: FROM
E-MAILS TO SELF-PUBLICATION

In 2007, following a series of political, sociological, and economic changes in Myanmar (or Burma), monks and pro-democracy activists led a series of demonstrations in Rangoon against the country's military regime. On 22 September 2007, the demonstrations escalated: In Rangoon 2,000 monks marched and in Mandalay, the second largest city of Burma, 10,000 demonstrated (Moe, 2007). The demonstrations, known as the "Saffron Revolution", involved tens of thousands of citizens across the country.

In Myanmar, privately owned newspapers had been banned since 1964. In 2013, the Ministry of Information temporarily permitted eight private daily newspapers (out of 17 that applied) to begin operating that same year. These newspapers included Khit Moe Daily, Shwe Naing Ngan Thit Daily, Union Daily, Empire Daily, the Messenger, Up-Date Daily, Myanmar Newsweek Daily, and Mizzima Daily, along with state-owned newspapers, magazines, and publishers (Petulla, 2013). During the uprisings, traditional media were controlled by the state (Chowdhury, 2008, 7).

Many international news organisations, including the BBC, were banned from setting foot in the country. Since 1999, the BBC had a Burmese correspondent based in Bangkok, Thailand. News organisations such as the BBC, the Japanese television network NHK, as well as the Associated Press set up their bureaux in Rangoon in 2013, as Burma opened its doors to the international press (Turvill, 2013). During the 2006 uprisings, Micheline Lévesque, programme agent at the now-defunct Canadian international human rights agency Rights & Democracy, said that Democratic Voice of Burma (DVB), a non-profit media organisation based in Oslo, Norway, lost a significant amount of expensive equipment during the Revolution and after Cyclone Nargis "due to seizures by the military and adverse conditions, including heavy rain" (Lévesque quoted in Pidduck, 2012, 542). For such organisations in Burma, "the dangers faced by DVB's fragile network of people and technology bring into relief the obstacles that must be taken into account in any discussion of the global flows of information that contribute to the contestation of authoritarian regimes" (Lévesque quoted in Pidduck, 2012, 542). BBC journalists also struggled to gather eyewitness accounts of events in Myanmar.

The Saffron Revolution is a case of increasing newsgathering with social media (Pidduck, 2012, 542). During the uprising in Myanmar, self-publication as a mode of storytelling highlighted the transformations occurring in the mode of communication of material sent to and sought by news organisations, including at the BBC (Chowdhury, 2008, 7).[1] User-generated content recorded on mobile phone cameras and camcorders "made its way into the mainstream press and broadcasting news media" (Cottle, 2010, 475). Laura Mottaz (2010) recalls that Burmese bloggers played a critical role as witnesses. Even "with limited Internet access, blog-gers found clever ways to circumvent government restrictions and send out updates about the protests. Many relied on foreign proxy servers and encrypted e-mails to keep their blogs updated during the protest" (Mottaz, 2010). For example,

> An anonymous blogger in Bangkok who went by the online name Jot-man went into Burma to talk to monks who were in hiding in safe houses. Jotman interviewed them and then posted the videos and their stories on his blog, sharing information that many traditional journal-ists couldn't get because the Burmese government is hostile to foreign journalists.
>
> (Glazer, 2010, 583)

Reports from Democratic Voice of Burma were also broadcasted back into Burma via satellite. "With international journalists banned from the country, these updates were the only source of information for protestors during the demonstrations" (Mottaz, 2010). In addition, protesters were able to send e-mails to "contact Burmese exiles, transnational advocacy net-works, and news agencies to relay information about the uprising" (Mottaz, 2010). Dissidents used chat services, Wikipedia, and Facebook to dissemi-nate information and several international news organisations, including *The New York Times* and the BBC, picked up on these eyewitness reports (Mottaz, 2010). In Myanmar, "citizen journalists, Internet cafe users inside Burma, pro-democracy bloggers from across the globe, and online newspa-pers based abroad" contributed to digital activism and reporting in profes-sional news organisations, including the Associated Press, Reuters, CNN, and the BBC (Chowdhury, 2008, 8–9).

As it had during the events of 7/7, the BBC received many pictures, vid-eos, texts, and e-mails from citizens, but this time, the citizens sending con-tent were located in Myanmar (Boaden, 2008; Holmes, 2007). One citizen in Rangoon told the BBC Burmese Service on Wednesday, 26 September: "When monks and people reached the mid-level platform of the Shwedagon Pagoda around 12:20 p.m., they [the police] closed the doors behind and riot police started to chase them and beat them up. Then about 200 were hauled off onto the trucks and driven away. About 80 monks were taken away" (Anonymous eyewitness, Rangoon cited in BBC, 2006b). "Riot police and soldiers are beating monks and other protesters at the east gate of Shwedagon Pagoda. They are starting a crackdown by all means. Police forces are stationed at Sule Pagoda as well. Regardless of this, just after noon, about 1,000 monks from a nearby monastery started a march to the Shwedagon Pagoda", wrote another citizen named Thila in Rangoon. On Thursday, 27 September, another anonymous witness shared with the BBC Burmese Service that soldiers "have shot several times into the crowd, one person was injured, they used tear gas. Now the injured person is being carried into a car to be taken to hospital. They (the soldiers) are using force on us" (Anonymous eyewitness, Rangoon cited in BBC, 2006b). An under-cover journalist who could not be named, because journalists were banned from the country, also reported for the news organisation from the sites of the events (BBC, 2006b). The BBC was able to verify and share with its audiences those anonymous and non-anonymous accounts of the events, particularly from Monday, 24 September, to Sunday, 29 September 2006.

The uprising in Myanmar and gathering of eyewitness accounts via social media took place at a particular moment in social networking history: At the time, Facebook was two years old with approximately 12 million users and Twitter had been created that same year. BBC journalists took advantage of the new possibilities social networks offered for newsgathering during the Myanmar insurrection. According to BBC journalists, it was the first noticeable instance in which BBC journalists sought information on social media such as Facebook, YouTube, and Flickr. Twitter had been created only months earlier and had not gained significant use as a tool of reportage. The UGC Hub filtered user-generated content in a coordinated way, suggesting that social networks had become integrated into newsgathering. For instance, Matthew Eltringham wrote, "we reported the Burma uprising of autumn 2007 through an equal mixture of content coming in directly to us and content we found on the Burmese blogs and social networks" (Eltringham, 2009, 55). Meanwhile, Vicky Taylor, BBC News Interactive, was working on Have Your Say, a section of the BBC News website dedicated to audience participation, as well as on the UGC Hub. She said that from the confines of the London Television Centre's 7th floor, UGC Hub journalists used social media to find sources and content during the uprisings: "Journalists now have to know how to seek out information and contact from all sorts of sources, and social network sites are key to this" (Taylor cited in Luft, 2008). Steve Herrmann, BBC Editor of the News website, also confirmed that the public broadcaster had published and curated text, pictures, audio, and video of citizens who had contacted the BBC News website and BBC Burmese service:

> We've also been looking at other sites and blogs, which are tracking the events—though this has become harder in the past 24 hours. But is this any different from the traditional role of a newsdesk–or an editor for that matter? I think there are some things, which have changed. Here are a few to start with: The newsgathering function suddenly has to broaden out to incorporate a lot more new potential sources. Major time and effort gets channelled into following up emails we've been sent, checking them out, contacting people back and getting their accounts published and on air.
>
> (Herrmann, 2007)

Rather than waiting to receive user-generated content from citizens (sent mainly to the BBC via e-mail) and managing that content, the BBC used the UGC Hub to seek user-generated content on the available social media platforms. Meanwhile,

> the Burmese junta managed to regain communication control relatively easily (only 1% of the Burmese population had access to the Internet). This was not before some of the most damaging images and accounts of brutal repression had been captured, circulated internationally and condemned by political leaders around the world.
>
> (Cottle, 2010, 477)

Collaboration between national and transnational networks, as well as the increasing role of ordinary citizen witnesses in mainstream news reportage, allowed for an alternative news logic showing the capability of news surveillance (Cottle, 2010, 478; see also Reese et al., 2007). Although the revolution did not result in the immediate democratisation of Burma (Chowdhury, 2008; Mottaz, 2010), the Saffron Revolution was not the only example of social media used for newsgathering.

Following the revolution, BBC journalists used social media for newsgathering and sourcing in other countries where BBC reporters had been banned, such as in Zimbabwe. Helen Boaden recalls, "On the day of the recent elections [in Zimbabwe], the BBC asked voters to text in and tell us their experiences at the polling booths. Those texts gave us a really broad diversity of experiences from right across the country" (Boaden, 2008). As a result of these events and a new self-publication context, the professional boundaries between social media and journalism managing this material became increasingly blurry. At the same time, these events demonstrated the complexity of conceptualising journalism and citizen journalism in crisis reporting.

Simultaneously, the UGC Hub gained preeminence within the BBC newsroom by developing and employing new newsgathering tactics. In October 2007, the UGC team expanded to 13 staff members and round-the-clock operations. As a response to the licence fee settlement, which required the BBC to cut approximately £155 million in annual news operation costs until the end of the Royal Charter period in 2016, the BBC merged radio, television, and online news into a converged multimedia newsroom.[2] Herrmann wrote, "[w]e've been moving all the journalists who work on the main online newsdesk from their traditional home on the seventh floor of BBC TV Centre in West London down to the main newsroom on the first and second floors" (Herrmann, 2008). This physical and structural transition started in April 2008 and was completed in June 2008, with the integration of the online news team in the newsroom (Allan and Thorsen, 2010, 33).

Meanwhile, the UGC Hub took its place in the middle of the newly converged multimedia newsroom. By positioning the UGC Hub in the centre of the newsroom, the BBC signalled both its desire to manage social media material centrally, and the importance of this nascent operation in the BBC's news production.[3] The move of the UGC Hub to the middle of the multimedia newsroom was also part of a larger institutional trend to cut overlapping processes within the news organisation and save money due to cuts in budget.[4]

The move of the UGC Hub from the seventh floor of the Television Centre in White City, London to the middle of the multimedia newsroom affected the relationship between the Hub and the rest of the newsroom. A news editor confirmed that "three years ago the online operation was on the seventh floor and people did not really talk to each other. Now, they are really at the heart of the newsroom".[5] Social media have been integrated into the work of journalists and managed by the UGC Hub, but this did not happen overnight: It is part of a larger process of structural change at the public broadcaster. In subsequent news events, BBC journalists learned how this new media could cohabit with traditional journalism. One major change in the BBC's journalistic process has been its reimagination of editorial guidelines. As social media material continued to be integrated in BBC reporting, journalists felt that they had to update their traditional guidelines to match the new digital reality.

NEW GUIDELINES: CEMENTING THE ROLE OF SOCIAL MEDIA IN JOURNALISM

Between 2009 and 2011, "news organisations gradually worked through the dilemmas associated with social media, and have published guidelines and undertaken training programmes on how to embrace these new formats whilst protecting their principles and brands" (Newman et al., 2011, 15). In 2008, the BBC was already taking official steps to manage social media to reassert its authority as a public broadcaster in the new media logic, and to cultivate symbolic boundaries with social media and its audiences. A similar trend involved the launch of the BBC social networking guidelines in March 2008. Kevin Bakhurst, former Controller of the BBC News channel and BBC News at One O'clock, attested that "[l]ike many established news providers, we have created an open and modern set of guidances to help our staff engage, gather news and spread their journalism, working within the BBC's editorial values that are at the core of our journalism" (Bakhurst, 2011). Similarly, Helen Boaden stated, "the new guidelines about what content BBC staff could put on social networking websites were designed to protect the corporation's brand" (Boaden paraphrased in Sweney, 2008b).

Four commandments directed the guidelines in social media dealings: engage in conversations and online conversations, do not "put the BBC into disrepute", trust users, and be open and transparent (BBC Social Networking Guidelines, 2008). The BBC asked its journalists to be mindful of the information they could disclose and to protect the reputation of the organisation. The guidelines brought up concerns about the idea of impartiality: "when forwarding or 're-tweeting' messages, care should be taken that it does not appear that the BBC is endorsing a particular opinion". The Corporation encouraged its journalists to add context when using social media. For instance, the guidelines stated, "add your own comment to the 'tweet' you have selected, making it clear why you are forwarding it, when you are speaking in your own voice and when you are quoting someone else's". The guidelines took into account issues of privacy and copyright. For instance, the guidelines prohibited journalists from using pictures they found on social media without the permission of the copyright owner. In early 2008, BBC managers sent these guidelines to all staff. Signalling that the Corporation was careful and serious about social media, the BBC asked journalists to follow official procedures tailored by senior figures within the news organisation.

The guidelines detailed what BBC journalists could or could not do within the context of British public broadcasting, which also affected the image of the BBC internationally. Helen Boaden said, "public and private space is complicated. People don't know when they put [pictures] up that [these pictures] could be used [in the media]" (Boaden in Sweney, 2008b). Boaden added that the guidelines made explicit that journalists would need to gain permission from right-holders before publishing photos found on social media sites. This is an example of journalists using the guidelines to articulate the boundaries of their work. It is also an example of a cultural transition: The line between social media and journalism was becoming less clear. At the same time, the BBC started a new logic: Social media and journalism are becoming part of a media logic involving structural, organisational, political, cultural, and economical changes in the media logic. Within this logic, actors have the ability to choose and shape social meanings, allowing changes in power relations and social meanings of journalism.

The transition in journalistic experiences with social media is illustrated by a senior manager's speech from that moment. Speaking at a Media Society[6] event, "Broadsheet vs. Broadband", in London, Pete Clifton, the BBC's Head of Editorial Development for Multimedia Journalism, reflected on this change in BBC journalism. Clifton suggested that after a period of learning about social media, the BBC had finally integrated social media into its journalism. He said,

> The day we just put those up without any questioning of whether that's right or not is the day we're in very serious trouble. It's gone through all the filters that our journalism would have gone through. It's quite labour intensive. We have another arm of our newsgathering operation—it can ultimately add to the richness of what we do, but we shouldn't take it lightly.
>
> (Clifton quoted in Oliver, 2008)

Subsequent crisis reporting events demonstrated the validity of Clifton's quote. These events reflect how deep normative meanings of journalistic structures, such as impartiality, foster a conception of new technologies as threats to the ideals of the profession. Journalists manage this by fostering journalistic autonomy and independence in new organisational forms.

THE MUMBAI ATTACKS: REASSESSING BBC NORMS[7]

From 26 to 29 November 2008, a series of attacks took place in Mumbai, India. These attacks, quickly dubbed "India's 9/11" (Allan, 2010, 332), were the work of Lashkar-e-Taiba (Soldiers of the Pure), a terrorist group based in Pakistan. Lashkar-e-Taiba is led by Hafiz Mohammad Saeed and fights against Indian control of Kashmir. From Pakistan, the terrorists travelled by boat across the Arabian Sea and reached Mumbai on 26 November, after which they divided into five groups, targeting five locations for their attacks (Indian Government, 2008; Neelamalar et al., 2009). The first target was Chhatrapati Shivaji Terminus railway station, the headquarters of Central Railways. Around 9:20 p.m., two terrorists, Mohammed Ajmal Amir Kasab and Ismail Khan, entered the station, firing their Kalashnikov rifles and lobbing grenades into the crowded main level. At 9:40 p.m., a similar scene unfolded at the iconic Leopold Café and Bar, a restaurant on Colaba Causeway, frequented by foreigners and Indians. Hafiz Arshad and Nasir fired and lobbed grenades into the café, then walked to the nearby five-star Taj Mahal Hotel, joining two other group members, Shoaib and Javed. Together, the group seized control of the hotel. Andreas Liveras, a 73-year-old, Cyprus-born British executive, spoke on his mobile phone to a BBC reporter while he was held hostage at the Taj. Later, he was caught and killed in a cross fire. At 10 p.m., Abdul Rehman Chotta and Fahadullah entered the five-star Oberoi Trident Hotel on Marine Drive and opened fire indiscriminately into the restaurant before taking hostages. That night, the Nariman Jewish community and outreach centre, commonly called Chabad House, also became a target. Babar Imran and Nazir fired guns outside before entering the fifth floor of the building, killing the rabbi and his pregnant spouse (Indian Government, 2008; Neelamalar et al., 2009). Alexander Wolfe, technology journalist and Editor in Chief of InformationWeek, wrote that

> Never before has a crisis unleashed so much raw data—and so little interpretation—than what we saw as the deadly terrorist attacks in Mumbai, India, unfolded. Amid the real-time video feeds (kudos to CNN International), cell phone pictures, and tweets, we were able to keep abreast of what seemed to be happening, and where it was going down, all the while not really knowing those other key, canonical components of journalistic information gathering—namely, who or why.
> (Wolfe, 2008)

Journalists and communication scholars considered the Mumbai attacks a "Twitter moment", because Twitter was inundated with tweets within minutes of the first attacks (Caulfield and Karmali, 2008; Jarvis, 2008). New media scholars such as Cherian George highlighted how the attacks have put the emergence of citizen journalism and user-generated content at the centre of news reporting (Lee, 2008). The coverage of the attacks "was notable for the ways in which ordinary citizens were able to express their anger and outrage at the obvious failure of political elites to prevent the attacks, despite warnings by intelligence agencies" (Sonwalkar, 2009). Stephanie Busari from CNN wrote that "with more than 6 million members worldwide, an estimated 80 messages, or 'tweets,' were being sent to Twitter.com via SMS every five seconds, providing eyewitness accounts and updates" (Bursari, 2008). Posts included offers of help for the media and updates on the situation. " 'One terrorist has jumped from Nariman house building to Chabad house—group of police commandos have arrived on scene,' one tweeter wrote" (Lee, 2008). In another example, "Neha Viswanathan, a former regional editor for Southeast Asia and a volunteer at Global Voices, told CNN, 'Even before I actually heard of it on the news I saw stuff about this on Twitter' " (Lee, 2008). The BBC's coverage of the Mumbai attacks in November 2008 highlights how citizen eyewitness accounts have had an impact on the social order of news production. Yet social media should not be reduced to events; they are part of a larger process of the organisation to become closer to its audiences.

This process provides insight on how the social order has both continued and evolved within the context of the BBC. When the story first broke on November 26, mainstream media sought material from social media. In Mumbai, people put their phones to use by posting photos and updates. On average, every five seconds, 70 tweets related to the attacks were posted on Twitter. For example, mumbaiattack tweeted, "Hospital update. Shots still being fired. Also, Metro cinema next door". Dupreee, self-described as a "computers, Internet, web 2.0, linux, open source, script-kiddin, tech-freak, music, guitars, rock, grunge, hip-hop. Go ahead, follow me. What do you have to lose?", tweeted, "Mumbai terrorists are asking hotel reception for room #s of American citizens and holding them hostage on one floor" (Beaumont, 2008; Busari, 2008). Jennifer Leggio from ZDNet reported that when the attacks happened, she and others could

> Do a Twitter Search for the hashtag #mumbai and you'll find thousands of tweets from folks near the site of the tragedy as well as folks in other countries who are offering support. People are sharing locations where blood is needed, police activity that they are witnessing, and the health status of their family and friends.
>
> (Leggio, 2008)

Journalists used Twitter and Flickr to share eyewitness accounts of the events (Busari, 2008). The BBC set up new pages on Wikipedia and Google

Maps, collaborating with its audiences by showing the key locations and buildings of the attacks, and linking to news stories and updates from citizens who had witnessed the unfolding events. "CNN's iReporters flooded the site with their videos and images of the terror attacks," said Busari (2008). Vinukumar Ranganathan, Chief Technological Officer at the Tata Institute of Social Sciences, took more than 100 pictures of the events and posted them on Flickr.[8] Bloggers used Metroblog,[9] a blog about the city of Mumbai, as a collective newswire and monitoring tool (Beaumont, 2008). Blogs, including MumbaiHelp, provided advice for people and families (Lee, 2008). Because many sources of information used to discuss the events were available to anyone with access to social media sites, mainstream news organisations took advantage by monitoring these sources.

> Major news organisations in India and around the globe struggled to cope with the amount of 'raw data' relayed via Twitter feeds, desperately trying to separate fact from conjecture for their live reports in what was fast becoming a curatorial role being defined under intense pressure.
>
> (Allan, 2013, 112)

The handling of these sources by BBC journalists highlights how the broadcaster negotiated its impartiality norm, a principle that has been under strain at the broadcasting organisation. This also highlights how journalists reasserted their journalistic independence towards the government and people using these emerging technologies.

Social media provided the opportunity for ordinary citizens and journalists to jointly report the unfolding stories (Murthy, 2011, 783). At the same time as the attacks took place, the BBC launched a webpage called "As it happened". The aim of this page was to provide news, analysis, description, and comments on breaking news stories as the events unfolded and the story developed. The page was formulated by a narrative involving journalists' eyewitness experiences on the ground, blogs' contents, links, selected Twitter feeds from audiences and journalists' accounts, and eyewitness evidence, such as video clips, images, voice clips, and news agencies' feeds (Gubbay, 2011). Through the "live feed", we recognise "multi-mediality" in the narrative structure as opposed to convergence news (Chouliaraki, 2010b, 9). The Mumbai terrorist attacks were a turning point in BBC journalism. They also provoked discussions involving tech-savvy journalists, audience members, and *The Independent* journalist Tom Sutcliffe on how the organisation should deal with social media with regard to accuracy and impartiality (Jones and Salter, 2012, 3).

During the attacks, under the leadership of Steve Herrmann, Editor of the BBC News website, the BBC incorporated social media into its journalistic practices and news stories. As recommended in the 2007 BBC report *From Seesaw to Wagon Wheel: Safeguarding Impartiality in the 21st Century*,[10] the BBC social media team monitored Twitter feeds, blogs, e-mails sent by viewers, media and official reports, news agencies, and other sources of information. Herrmann recalls,

> As for the Twitter messages we were monitoring, most did not add a great amount of details to what we knew of events, but among other things they did give a strong sense of what people connected in some way with the story we thinking and seeing. 'Appalled at the foolishness of the curious onlookers who are disrupting the NSG operations,' wrote one. 'Our soldiers are brave but I feel we could have done better,' said another. There was assessment, reaction and comment there and in blogs. . . . All this helped to build up a rapidly evolving picture of a confusing situation.
>
> (Herrmann, 2008)

The coverage of the Mumbai attacks on the live update page "As it happened" provides insight into interactions and conceptualisations of impartiality at the public broadcaster. Herrmann acknowledged the risks associated with using material from accounts that had not been checked. During the attacks, BBC journalists added new information from these sources to the live update page "As it happened". Herrmann wrote,

> Our aim with these pages—we did something similar during the U.S. election—is to provide news, analysis, description, and comment in short snippets as soon as it becomes available. It is a running account, where we are making quick judgments on and selecting what look like most relevant and informative bits of information as they come in, rather than providing the more considered version of events we are able to give in our main news stories of the day.
>
> (Herrmann, 2008)

At the BBC, the coverage of the Mumbai attacks was the first live crisis news update webpage experience. Herrmann said that the accounts on the website pushed journalists to

> move more quickly and include a wider array of perspectives and sources, not all verified by us, but all attributed, so that in effect we leave some of the weighing up to each bit of information and context to you . . . as time compressed, decision-making, selection and judgement had to be made fast.
>
> (Herrmann, 2008)

In this remark, Herrmann acknowledged that the BBC published unfiltered and unverified social media information on the live page. It left the audience to decide whether the BBC reporters-curated information was accurate or authentic, reflecting a vision in conflict with the wagon wheel approach and the Editorial Guidelines.

On the second day of the attacks, a thread of tweets caused confusion at the BBC. One tweet stated that the Indian government was trying to silence journalists and Twitter, either by blocking the social media from the country or by asking Twitter to filter out tweets related to Mumbai, out of fear that the coverage might help the gunmen (Government of India, 2008; Sweney, 2008). Lloyd Shepperd, an Australian blogger, added this unconfirmed report to his blog, and the BBC sourced this information from his blog and posted it on its live page at 11:08 a.m.: "1108 Indian government asks for live Twitter updates from Mumbai to cease immediately. 'ALL LIVE UPDATES—PLEASE STOP TWEETING about #Mumbai police and military operations', a tweet says". The story appeared on the BBC live event page along with other sources such as journalists' first accounts of the events and bloggers' comments. Other news organisations, including CNN, also published the inaccurate tweet on their websites (Busari, 2008). There was no official source for the information; a blogger had merely found another tweet making this claim. Later the same day, the Indian government officially confirmed that this tweet was only a rumour. By that point, the BBC had already published the tweet on its live blog page, and in doing so had mistakenly circulated unverified and inaccurate information.

In the United Kingdom, the BBC's posting of this tweet on its website prompted reactions from journalists and BBC audiences. On 2 December, Tom Sutcliffe (2008), a journalist for *The Independent* and, since 2011, a presenter for BBC Radio 4, wrote that the BBC was playing a risky game with impartiality by using social media during live coverage of the attacks. Evaluating the work of the BBC in his column on the online version of *The Independent*, Sutcliffe wrote,

> Given that several 'Tweets' instructively contradicted the official line on what was happening you might argue that this enlistment of an army of virtual stringers improved the BBC's coverage . . . But that argument wouldn't take account of the subtle alteration of trust that takes place when you read coverage that cuts and pastes random 'Tweets' alongside more conventional forms of BBC journalism.
>
> (Sutcliffe, 2008)

His post argued that social media represented a threat to the Corporation's news coverage. Sutcliffe wrote, "[g]iven that several 'tweets' instructively contradicted the official line on what was happening, you might argue that this enlistment of an army of virtual stringers improved BBC's coverage", but "they'll pass on rumour as readily as a fact, and there is absolutely no way of telling which is which" (Sutcliffe, 2008).

On 4 December 2008, Herrmann (2008b) posted a blog entry, "Mumbai, Twitter and Live Updates", on The Editors blog, and audience views were overwhelmingly similar to those of Sutcliffe. BBC audience members demonstrated their desire for the BBC to keep its reputation of accuracy and balance. Many commentators also pointed out the risk of the BBC running unverified material and the impact it could have on the BBC's reputation. Chris Haynes commented, "I was concerned at the time, and I am still concerned, at the inclusion of Twitter-sourced material in your 'main' story. This is, journalistically speaking, very dangerous" (Haynes in Herrmann, 2008b). rjmhome wrote, "The BBC is becoming increasingly lazy and reports what other reporters and miscellaneous vox pop are saying rather than relying on its own considerable resources to publish the facts after checking them" (rjmhome in Herrmann, 2008b). real de madrid wrote,

> You are using a news source that is not verifiable. Someone could be sitting in a wine bar in Kent and send a Tweet alleging he just witnessed something that is happening on the other side of the world. The use of such unreliable (to put it mildly) information is only acceptable on the BBC Sports website in their live ticker on the day the transfer deadline closes.
>
> (real de madrid in Herrmann, 2008b)

Former BBC international correspondent Alfred Hermida said that the BBC justified this practice on the grounds that there was a case "for simply monitoring, selecting and passing on the information we are getting as quickly as we can, on the basis that many people will want to know what we know and what we are still finding out" (Hermida, 2010, 300). Facing criticism for allowing unverified and inaccurate material on the BBC website, Herrmann (2008) wrote that it was up to readers to decide how much credence they gave to individual sources. Herrmann added, "some of the many e-mails we received and the follow-up contacts contributed directly to our reporting, with first-hand accounts of the events, including that of Andreas Liveras, who was, sadly, later killed in the violence" (Herrmann, 2008). In response to this comment, Cellan-Jones replied, "if this story does turn out to be a myth it will be a handy reminder to treat everything you hear on a social network with a degree of scepticism" (Cellan-Jones, 2008). In this series of interactions, Cellan-Jones and Herrmann suggested that there was a time when what we now call "mainstream media" existed not to provide a conversation, but to be there first with the news. He also added that

> What Twitter has done is to provide instant information about anything that is happening near its millions of users, coupled with a brilliant way of sharing that information. What it doesn't do is tell us what is true and what isn't—and that makes the work of mainstream media outlets and professional reporters all the more relevant.
>
> (Cellan-Jones, 2008)

Rory Cellan-Jones, a BBC Technology correspondent, wrote that as useful as social media are, the BBC still needs a robust newsgathering operation of its own. Cellan-Jones's reaction is telling: He shows how journalists are taking opportunities to reaffirm their journalistic independence online. Cellan-Jones stated, "the role of mainstream media to report fact over fiction has been made even more relevant in the digital era" (Cellan-Jones cited in Sweney, 2008). Later, Herrmann responded to Sutcliffe, acknowledging that the BBC should have checked the information online:

> Should we have checked this before reporting it? Made it clearer that we hadn't? We certainly would have done if we'd wanted to include it in our news stories (we didn't) or to carry it without attribution. In one sense, the very fact that this report was circulating online was one small detail of the story that day. But should we have tried to check it and then reported back later, if only to say that we hadn't found any confirmation? I think in this case we should have, and we've learned a lesson. The truth is, we're still finding out how best to process and relay such information in a fast-moving account like this.
>
> (Herrmann, 2008b)

Much like other crisis events in the history of the BBC such as the crisis of 1926,[11] the Mumbai events provided the BBC with an opportunity to reflect on impartiality and the future of the independence of its organisation; the attacks also provided tech-savvy journalists such as Herrmann with an opportunity to renegotiate journalistic meanings and social processes. As Stuart Allen writes, "Users gain insight into how a major story is being put together, even when it entails having to accept some responsibility for assessing the quality—and reliability—of the information being processed" (2013, 116). Meanwhile, in their online publications, other news organisations such as *The Guardian* and journalism.co.uk reported the BBC admitting its mistake on its blog. This trend showed how British media and journalism circles took this story seriously.[12]

Post-Mumbai, the BBC developed impartiality with a renewed set of features. The emergence of social media and its new logic of communication have allowed tech-savvy journalists such as Herrmann to gain knowledge of social media and play a strategic role in the configuration of impartiality. The analysis of that moment of crisis suggests that the organisation strived to keep its impartiality and accuracy norms, to remain trusted by its audiences. The organisation also aligned its reporting to new forms of action (see also Jones and Salter, 2012). However, citizen material found on social media is part of the BBC's daily news activities centralised in the UGC Hub. The centralisation of social media activities as UGC Hub responsibilities indicates that BBC journalism is transforming. It also shows how social media are increasingly taken seriously by the public broadcaster to protect journalistic ethics.

In the Mumbai case, social media play an increasingly significant role in defining BBC impartiality. Since the emergence of social media post-7/7, tech-savvy journalists who understand and work with new formats of social media and other information technology have become more important in the newsroom. Tech-savvy journalists have played a major role in redefining impartiality at the BBC. Post-Mumbai, we see these journalists developing further tactics (verification, contextualisation, and openness) to bolster impartiality.

The processes of fact checking and verification show that since the Mumbai attacks of 2008 techies have renegotiated the meaning of impartiality in their daily activities. For example, the BBC UGC Hub, which has been located strategically at the centre of the multimedia newsroom since 2007, allows journalists to verify social media information before publishing it on BBC outlets. After verifying the source, the Hub communicates user-generated content via an intranet linking BBC departments. Journalists at the Hub have also developed rigorous verification processes. At the BBC, verification refers to two main practices: accuracy over speed and forensic verification practices. For accuracy over speed, the Editorial Guidelines ask journalists to apply "due accuracy" in their reporting first before publishing social media content. For instance, in contrast with the way BBC journalists handled social media during the Mumbai attacks coverage, Eltringham argued that journalists should always verify social media material by checking every image, video, or source before broadcasting the content:

> We always check out each and every image, video or key contact before we broadcast them, to make sure they are genuine and to resolve any copyright issues. When it's impossible to do that—such as with content sent from Iran or Burma—when contacting the contributors is very hard to do or might put them in danger, we interrogate the images, using BBC colleagues who know the area and the story to help identify them.
> (Matthew Eltringham quoted in McAthy, 2010)

Reflecting Eltringham's vision, a reporter said that journalists have to be careful with any kind of social media:

> After the death of Michael Jackson, TMZ was the first website to break the story. Then, it started trending on Twitter. But, certainly as a correspondent I automatically go to Facebook or Bebo. When you do that, you have first to go to the process of what you can or not get. . . . Because we are a public broadcaster we have a duty to go one step further to be absolutely sure that we can use these pictures and we have all the permissions. Because people pay for us and they have no choice, we have the legal obligation to do so. . . . You have to be very careful with any kind of social media and check the veracity of it before publishing the information through BBC outlets [sic].[13]

This means that for the BBC, journalism was not simply about breaking the news; it was about getting the right news first. In addition to being good journalism, verifying first is also a way for journalists to differentiate themselves from the competition. For example, several journalists mentioned ways that BBC's verification practices diverge from those of other news organisations, particularly Sky News. In its verification practices, the BBC has positioned its journalism in the new media logic. Here we see practices ushered in by tech-savvy journalists; we also see the BBC Editorial Guidelines (2011) being rearticulated in a set of editorial decisions.

The changing structure of the newsroom enables journalists to get the news right rather than get it first. Techies have played a crucial role in the process. For example, the formation of the BBC UGC Hub (in 2005), coupled with its location at the centre of the multimedia newsroom (between 2007 and 2008), has facilitated journalistic verifications of social media information before publishing the stories on BBC outlets. The UGC Hub communicates social media content through an intranet that disseminates information to BBC departments and notifies them when information has been validated. "Whoever is compiling the live page can visualise all the approved contents and decide to publish them", said Nathalie Malinarich, World Editor at the BBC News website (quoted in Bruno, 2011). The UGC Hub has "developed an incredibly sophisticated and nuanced understanding of the 'who, what, when, where and why' of 'social newsgathering' or, put another way, 'finding good stuff on the web'", said Eltringham (2010). In the same vein, a female foreign correspondent added, "if we have floods, we receive pictures. The first thing that we would ask is if anybody has it on their mobile. And so we will get those and download those from people".[14] The BBC UGC Hub is the central unit responsible for deciding what social media material is valid or not in the newsroom. "UGC and verification are no longer a side operation . . . They have become part of the journalistic toolbox, alongside agency pictures, field reporters, background interviews. It's critical for any big newsroom that wants credibility in storytelling", stated Chris Hamilton, BBC Social Media Editor (quoted in Turner, 2012).

The Hub and BBC journalists have also used forensic verification practices. These practices include comparing social media content with existing material, using the expertise of the BBC Newsgathering operation to produce the news, and using traditional journalistic practices such as sourcing or phone calls. UGC journalists use a comparative strategy by cross-referencing newly received material with existing material. This process includes lateral and technical checks.

The expressions "lateral and technical checks" was used by Chris Hamilton on the panel, "Verification, rumours and corrections, discussing best practices", presented at news:rewired on 13 July 2012, digital media events from Journalism.co.uk. Lateral checks include: (a) Referencing locations against maps and existing images from geo-located images, (b) Maintaining lists of previously verified material to act as reference for colleagues covering the stories, (c) Checking weaponry, vehicles, and licence plates against plates known for the given country, (d) Examining weather reports and shadows to confirm that the conditions shown fit with the claimed date and time,

(e) Asking: are other people in the location saying the same thing?, (f) Asking: does the story match up with what everybody else is saying?, (g) Asking: is this a repost? Technical checks include image verification and raise the following questions: Who owns the copyright? Are there signs of editing? What is the video quality? Is this too good to be true (Murray, 2011)?

The sets of questions asked in lateral and technical checks are specific to social media uses. Techies have developed these questions as they acquired a more acute understanding of social media tools. In a sense, these practices are not new; what is new is the combination of those practices in social media contexts.

UGC Hub journalists also analyse social media material through the newsgathering expertise of the BBC. Journalists use the expertise of the BBC World Service, BBC Monitoring, and BBC UGC Hub. For example, journalists are "working with our colleagues in BBC Arabic and BBC Monitoring to ascertain that accents and language are correct for the location" (Murray, 2011). The expertise of journalists and newsgathering local knowledge enables journalists to understand accents and nuances in language. Murray notes, "I can't tell a western Libyan accent from an eastern one, but I know that there's at least one colleague an email away who can. Likewise, when it comes to telling Homsi from Damascene dialect, there are people who can bring that knowledge to the process" (Murray, 2011). The UGC Hub team verifies user-generated content received through social media from a variety of sources, with differing agendas, reputations, and levels of credibility. Alex Murray provides the following example:

> Around 3 p.m. on 23 February, we were asked to verify video claiming to show bodies in the morgue of Al-Jalaa hospital in Benghazi. BBC Monitoring was able to confirm that the accents were eastern Libyan, what the captions and voices were saying, and to give context to the likely date of the events. By 6 p.m., this verified material was in the system in time for the Six O'clock News on BBC1 and the BBC News Channel, as well as BBC World News and our website.
>
> (Murray, 2011)

Journalists also say that they use traditional journalistic practices to make sure they get the right story. These include speaking to the source to ask the 5W questions—who, what, where, why, when, how—and conducting background checks to verify individuals and facts. UGC journalists consult experts on date verification to search for the original source of content uploads and sequences (Murray, 2011). James Morgan, a broadcast journalist, describes the process as he observed it during the 2010 Haiti earthquake news coverage:

> We can start from the mobile number prefix, but we can also check the IP address from where they send us an email. It depends on the

instances. The best way to authenticate is to talk with the people and if they are not legitimate they very quickly stumble. You ask a combination of factual things that we can corroborate and then more open questions. So you can have answers like: 'There's a supermarket in front of me, which collapsed, people are leaving the buildings.' As soon as we feel this guy is for real, the first thing we do is, we have a network system here, a kind of intranet, it's called the NPS, we use it to flash a message, very short, just say: Haiti, eyewitness, the name of the person and some other details. But, we don't publish his number, we just flash it. And when the colleagues on radio, TV and web operations see this, they phone us and ask: 'Can we have his telephone number please?'.

(James Morgan quoted in Bruno, 2011)

Tech-savvy journalists' verification practices have become engrained as features of BBC impartiality in all the Corporation's reporting, reflecting how in times of crisis the BBC has reaffirmed an old norm in a new form (see also Philips, 2010).

The new media logic led to a second enhanced feature of impartiality: contextualisation. When a journalist creates a story, s/he asks the 5W questions to develop context and analysis. As a story evolves, these questions become more specific. In a social media context, journalists add value to the multiple voices on the Internet by contextualising and analysing. For instance, a journalist can call a social media source to ask a question and add context to the social media information. Techies have developed editorial tactics such as labelling and linking to online sources. In a blog post, Herrmann suggests not using Twitter: Journalists should rely on facts, labelling, and keeping social media information separate from journalistic material (Herrmann in Newman, 2009, 9). Labelling involves stating the source of the information, such as a social media source or a website online (such as Twitter and/or Facebook) or on the radio or TV.[15]

When journalists tweet, they can also add value by contextualising their tweets. For example, Jon Williams (@JonWilliams), World Newsgathering Editor, tweeted about the stoning of an Afghan couple in 2011: "After 1st public stoning in Afghanistan since 2001 we revisit story of a couple executed for adultery by Taliban http://bbc.in/cLL6he" (January 2011). Williams added multimedia value and context to the tweet. Reporters are successful when they are able to create new newsroom routines through the introduction of new technologies (see also Usher, 2012). The BBC Trust[16] also encourages contextualisation as a journalistic practice in social media (BBC Trust, 2012). From the point of view of the Trust (and journalists), the role of shoe-leather journalism remains important: It distinguishes the BBC from the voices found on social media platforms.

The third feature of impartiality is openness. This feature refers to institutional transparency during production. For example, a group of techies and managers developed an editorial policy requiring journalists to acknowledge their mistakes by following a series of steps. When a journalist posts a tweet containing erroneous information, the tweet will remain on the thread. Instead of deleting the tweet, the journalist generates a new tweet to supplement the original (erroneous) information, acknowledging the mistake or adding new information to the tweet, reflecting the *From Seesaw to Wagon Wheel* vision of how to handle corrections. This practice of openness is not unique to the BBC. At competing websites, such as that of *The Guardian*, journalists acknowledge errors at the bottom of selected journalistic articles. Similarly, the BBC guidelines for Twitter state that if journalists make mistakes, they must own up to the error, apologise, and make any necessary corrections. For instance, Sophie Brendel (@sophiebr), Head of Digital Communications, did not delete an erroneous tweet she had earlier posted; instead, she tweeted, "Apologies, previous tweet on BBC Online outage contained the wrong link. Correcting now" (13 July 2012).

The BBC also runs online platforms discussing news production transparently. For example, launched on 26 June 2006 with an inaugural blog post by Helen Boaden, Director of News, The Editors blog enables BBC senior editors to discuss issues in news production (Boaden, 2006). The example below illustrates the process of transparency in news production. In May 2012, for approximately 90 minutes, the BBC News website featured a picture supposedly of the Syrian massacre in Houla. In reality, that picture was taken a decade earlier in Iraq by Marco Di Lauro, a professional photographer working for Getty Images who "nearly feel out of his chair" when he saw his picture on the BBC website. As he later stated, "What I am really astonished by is that a news organisation like the BBC doesn't check the sources and it's willing to publish any picture sent it by anyone: activist, citizen journalist or whatever" (Di Lauro in Furness, 2012). Activists in Syria sourced this picture and posted it on Twitter; the BBC published the picture with a label, a disclaimer that the image could not be verified. When it became clear that the photo was tagged incorrectly, Hamilton published an account of the process leading up to posting the picture on The Editors blog (Hamilton, 2012). If the source of information cannot be confirmed prior to publication, journalists can label and describe the source because the news retains public service value. Max Fisher, former writer and editor at *The Atlantic*, and now foreign affairs blogger at *The Washington Post*, wrote,

> The BBC's error seems like an innocent one, and is in some ways an inevitable result of the changing ways in which international media cover conflict zones. Places such as Houla, where Syrian forces killed dozens of civilians including 32 children under the age of 10, are often too dangerous to cover first-hand. Even when journalists can make their way in, as with *New York Times* photographer Tyler Hicks' trip to Syria in February, the visit must be brief, and even the journey to and

from can be enormously risky; Times reporter Anthony Shadid died on the trip.

(Fisher, 2012)

Chris Hamilton, BBC's Social Media Editor, added that in some instances, journalists still use the citizen material and make their doubts clear. Steve Herrmann writes that in some occasions,

> When we have done all we can to check but still cannot be 100% sure, we will sometimes still decide to use the material, whilst making these doubts clear, and the Trust is now asking us to be more consistent in the way we signpost and caveat this type of content. In those rare cases where we do get something wrong, we acknowledge and correct it as soon as we can.

(Herrmann, 2012)

In social media contexts, the BBC reaffirmed their impartiality by continuing old practices in new forms, using verification, contextualisation, and transparency. But this does not mean that journalists routinely share all the details on how stories are found and selected; nor does it mean they share how sources are selected and verified. For example, a minority of journalists use The Editors blog to feature the inner workings of the newsroom. Numerous studies suggest an increase in journalistic transparency practices through journalistic engagement in discussion about their work on social networks (Larsosa et al., 2012). These practices are engrained in journalistic practices and norms in crisis reporting.

Verification and fact checking are features of contemporary journalism as an Anglo-American invention (Chalaby, 1998). Practices such as lateral checks are strategies that tech-savvy journalists have developed over time through the UGC Hub. In times of crisis reporting, journalists have understood impartiality through the prism of old values and practices. The use of social media in crisis reporting has enabled the BBC to maintain its professional boundaries by reinforcing the norm of impartiality and by highlighting a set of new practices and norms. Journalists construct meanings around social media. When there is a threat to their journalistic integrity, they create new structures and norms. At the same time, more citizens are now part of crisis news production processes.

THE IRANIAN ELECTIONS: TWITTER AND REAL TIME JOURNALISM

While the BBC gradually integrated social media practices into its newsgathering and sourcing, eight months following the Mumbai attacks, another important crisis news event highlighted the increasing relevance of social media in BBC journalism. On 12 June 2009, Iran held its presidential election. The 2009 Iran election story was a turning point in social media and journalism, "not just in terms of content turning to BBC News but tapping into the story", particularly in terms of using Twitter as a newsgathering tool.[17] Journalistic coverage of the presidential election was different from that of previous elections. The events in Iran in 2009 show how journalists used social media in newsgathering, research, and reporting of news. Indeed, BBC News correspondents started employing Twitter widely during the Iranian election, mainly as a newsgathering tool.

In the presidential election of 12 June 2009, for the first time since 1979, more than 80% of Iranians voted (Ghanavizi, 2011, 262). Since 2004, Iranian blogs have become very popular, following the country's high levels of literacy and education, and young people's efforts to connect to the Internet (Ghanavizi, 2011, 258). During the election, blogs became an important public space to discuss the importance of participation in opposition parties and to promote change in the Ahmadinejad government (Ghanavizi, 2011, 262). As the Iranian government realised the social impact of the Internet, it undertook more stringent efforts to control the Internet. During this time, the government filtered more than five million websites, social networks like Facebook, and blogs. Many dissident bloggers were imprisoned for criticising the government and its policies (Ghanavizi, 2011, 263).

The U.S. State Department asked social networking service Twitter to delay a network upgrade scheduled for the day of the election, to protect the interests of Iranians who would want to communicate during the election. "Twitter Inc said in a blog post it delayed a planned upgrade because of its role as an 'important communication tool in Iran.' The hour-long maintenance was put back to 5 p.m. EDT/2100 GMT, which corresponds to 1:30 a.m. on Wednesday in Iran", confirmed Sue Pleming at Reuters (2009). Twitter thus moved the upgrade to Wednesday, 10 June at 1:30 a.m. in Tehran (Grossman, 2009). The election was held on Friday, 12 June. Mahmoud Ahmadinejad won the election with 62% of the votes. His nearest opponent, Mir-Hossein Mousavi received 34% of the votes. And because of irregularities in the results, Iranians protested in the streets of Iranian cities and around the world in cities with large Iranian populations. Meanwhile, Twitter exploded with tweets in English and Farsi.

Iranian government officials continued to put heavy restrictions on BBC journalists reporting in the country. Internet censorship in Iran included the blockage of sites such as Flickr, MySpace, YouTube, and Facebook (Mortensen, 2011, 8). Government authorities also jammed satellite signals and confiscated protesters' recording devices, including mobile phones (Mortensen, 2011). In the same vein, evidence from academic research shows that authorities, including soldiers, increasingly target journalists to stop them from reporting (Allan, 2013, 178; Allan and Zelizer, 2004; Ghanavizi, 2011; Hoskins and O'Loughlin, 2010; Seib, 2010; Tumber, 2010).

Numerous restrictions by the Iranian government prompted BBC reporters to turn to social media to cover the events. The Iranian Ministry of Culture and Islamic Guidance said that journalists were "not allowed to cover 'unauthorised gatherings' or move around freely in Tehran—though there are no controls over what they can say" (Herrmann, 2009). This meant that journalists had to cover the events from their bureaux and not from the streets of Iran, wrote Jon Williams (2009). A broadcast journalist's statement supports Williams's comment. In an interview, the journalist said that in Tehran, no telephone lines and Internet connections were available for most of the day.[18] As a result, she had a difficult time finding eyewitness accounts. Jon Williams, BBC World Newsgathering Editor, also noted,

> We're supposed to only operate from our bureau and not to report from the streets. It was a disappointing development and one that means that we're now operating under formal 'reporting restrictions.' While John Simpson and Jon Leyne are prevented from traveling to opposition rallies, and must seek permission to attend something like Friday prayers, there are no 'minders' sitting on their shoulder with a red pen, deciding what they can and cannot say.
>
> (Williams, 2009)

As the protests grew, the Iranian government ran an intensified technical filtering system. The Revolutionary Guard enforced Internet content standards and blocked Facebook and Twitter. The Iranian government jammed BBC satellite signals used to broadcast BBC Persian TV:

> Since Friday 12 June the BBC Persian service, other BBC services, and the services of other broadcasters on Hotbird 6 have been subject to deliberate interference. . . . BBC Arabic television and various language services have also been experiencing transmission problems including being off the air at various points. The satellite operator has traced the interference and has confirmed it is coming from within Iran. . . . Online was partially blocked since 2006.
>
> (BBC, 2009b)

BBC satellite technicians stated that they located this interference in Iran (BBC, 2009b). World Service Director Peter Horrocks added, "[t]here has been intermittent interference from Iran since Friday, but this is the heaviest yet" (Horrocks, 2010). "Since the presidential protests, the government has realised the power of that footage and decided to work actively to not let the BBC and others broadcast it", said Sanam Dolatshahi, Producer and Presenter for BBC Persian TV (Dolatshahi quoted in Halliday, 2011). Throughout the election, Iranian officials distorted events. Dolatshani mentioned that Iranian officials "would jam our footage and show their own version of events—using the same UGC, but to tell a different story, a different version of events. They would also try to make us broadcast wrong stuff so that we would lose our credibility" (Dolatshahi quoted in Halliday, 2011).

All of these conditions created challenges for BBC reporters who were trying to cover the election in Iran.[19] However, it was difficult for the Guard to consistently enforce content standards. First, Twitter was more difficult to monitor or censor because it is a multiheaded platform. Second, people outside Iran uploaded content onto social networks sites (Newman, 2009). Third, many Iranians learned to circumvent the regime's censorship by using proxy servers. Using data from AnchorFree, a widely used virtual private network (VPN) distributor, Elizabeth Flock (2012) from *The Washington Post* reported that in 2012 Iranians used 10 times more VPN services than in 2011. In July 2011, 35,505 people in Iran used VPN services and in January 2012, 366,403 people used these services. "In Egypt, . . . usage spiked in August, the same month that the nation's military retook Tahrir Square from protesters. VPNs hit their highest usage in Syria last month, as violence between the government and protesters escalates", noted Flock (2012). As in previous cases of audience participation, in Iran in 2009 citizens captured the events using mobile phones and digital cameras. Unlike in previous protests in Iran, web-savvy protesters uploaded footage to video-sharing websites such as YouTube, social media platforms, and the websites of mainstream news organisations (Newman, 2009). These trends revealed the limited effectiveness of censorship efforts by the Iranian government during the 2009 election. However, it is important to note that Iranian Internet access remains in the hands of a small percentage of the population (Mortensen, 2011, 8), which suggests that reporting would be skewed towards the people who are connected and able to manage online communication.

As a result of these logistical challenges, BBC reporters employed social media in two distinct ways: as a tool of newsgathering and as a way for audiences to participate in news production, reflecting the increasing "collaboration" between journalists and "ordinary" citizen witnessing in news production. Peter Horrocks, BBC World Service Director, wrote that "the availability of witness material from Iran is enabling international news organisations to be able to report the story. Viewers of BBC Persian TV have been in touch (in Farsi), sending videos, stills and providing personal accounts" (Horrocks, 2010). Throughout the events, the BBC asked audiences to participate in the coverage of the events. The BBC sought material online and received contributions from audiences through the e-mail address yourpics@bbc.co.uk the BBC's upload video function, comments on Have Your Say, and HYS on Twitter (Horrocks, 2010). Reflecting the changing balance of power of journalists and citizens, journalists at the BBC stated that

> UGC was valuable in helping report the story, but it goes beyond that because it gives a direct relationship between the service and the people

of Iran and it gives them a level of engagement, a level of authenticity, which you wouldn't get from conventional television coverage. So actually they've been able to turn a disadvantage into an advantage in that way.

(Richard Sambrook quoted in Newman, 2009)

BBC journalists sought images, videos, and citizen accounts of the events on social media platforms. Journalists searched for images on Flickr's Iran feed, Picassa, and the weblog Tehran live. They also found videos on Youtube, especially on the account profiles of ahriman46, iranlover100, and persianlover2007. Journalists also used blogs to follow the story. Most of the blogs journalists used as sources were institutional in nature. The institutional blogs that BBC reporters used as sources included *The Huffington Post*; the Islamic Republic of Iran Broadcasting (IRIB) channel PressTV blog; the 24-hour Iranian news network; *The Guardian; The New York Times*; Global Voices, the citizen-led website run by the Berkman Centre at Harvard University; the expat blog Tehran Bureau; the blog of Gary Sick, U.S. Iran expert at the Middle East Institute and adjunct professor at the School of International and Public Affairs (SIPA) at Columbia University; and the blog of Juan Cole, professor of history at the University of Michigan. Journalists still relied on traditional journalistic strategies used to define newsworthiness, such as references to powerful sources based on past credentials to report the news. The use of blogs in Iran is not surprising: In Iran, "bloggers have for years been rated as the most trustworthy source of news because they have been difficult to control by the Islamic government" (Cottle, 2010, 584).

In the 2009 Iranian election, social media activities took place particularly on Twitter. An important feature of Twitter is the hashtag (#)—a labelling convention helping users to pull together tweets on a topic, placed before relevant keywords or sentences, with no spaces, to categorise a tweet. Hashtags allowed users to search for tweets using a range of specific and broad terms, both on Twitter and on Internet search engines. During the Iranian election, the most popular hashtag was #Iranelections49. If users clicked on the hashtag, a list of tweets that include the hashtag appeared. Twitter became a major aggregating tool for breaking news and pictures. Journalists at the BBC used Twitter to gather leads, sources, and the latest news; they also put it to use as a distribution tool. The Iranian restriction had a limited impact on journalism, because Iranians under 30, which represent two-thirds of the population, are tweeting and blogging:

While we've used Twitter for information on previous stories, such as the Hudson plane crash, it's the protest in Iran that has seen it become mainstream, providing real-time commentary on events in Tehran and elsewhere—events which we're banned from attending, but which we can follow 'online'. . . . members of the new generation in Iran are 'wired' in a way their parents, who lived through the Iranian Revolution 30 years ago, could never have imagined. So while the authorities in Tehran are trying to limit just how much we can see and hear, technology opens a window on what's going on.

(Williams, 2009)

Similarly, social media were probably the only way that journalists could report this election:

UGC was valuable in helping report the story, but it goes beyond that because it gives a direct relationship between the service and the people of Iran and it gives them a level of engagement, a level of authenticity, which you wouldn't get from conventional television coverage. So actually they've been able to turn a disadvantage into an advantage in that way. From 7 June until 26 June they record 2,024,266 tweets about the election in Iran. Approximately 480,000 users contributed to the conversation. 59.3 per cent of the users just tweeted once—and they contributed 14.1 per cent of the total number. The top 10 per cent of users accounted for 65.5 per cent of total tweets. One in four tweets about Iran was re-tweeted of another user's content.

(Sambrook, 2010, 92)

Social media were essential in the construction of BBC news stories. Jon Leyne, a BBC correspondent, was expelled from the country and, from his desk in London, turned to social media sources to put stories together (Sambrook, 2010, 91). The BBC's Persian TV reported from outside Iran, because it had been banned from the country since 2009 (Holmwood and Dehghan, 2009). Persian TV developed its stories with contributions from SMS, emails, and images from viewers.[20]

During the Iranian election, journalists solicited updates on social media rather than simply managing the information sent to them by e-mail. More than just an addition to reporting, social media were central in reporting the election in Iran. The growing number of breaking news stories requiring the use of social media created a need for new social media positions at the BBC.

Social media created a new set of questions for journalists. In the coverage of the presidential election, journalists took into account the lack of balance among social media participants to sustain the norm of impartiality. Many participants on Twitter favoured the leading opposition candidate, Mousavi, whose supporters were often younger, more computer-literate, and better connected to the Western community in Iran and Iranian exile communities in the West. Steve Herrmann, BBC Online Editor, wrote that "the majority of messages on Twitter, both within Iran and abroad, are from Mousavi sympathisers—a factor we need to allow for. There's no filter or editorial process other than the capacity of those involved to correct or contradict each other" (Herrmann, 2009).[21] Reflecting this tendency for

Mousavi sympathisers, a journalist from the Today Programme stated that the BBC's Persian service had received thousands of emails, but found difficulty finding Ahmadinejad supporters for its interactive programmes:

> Turi Munthe, CEO of the citizen journalism website Demotix, spells out the dangers: All the blogging, the twittering, the Facebook activity . . . is from a self-selecting demographic—media switched on, westernised, reformist. We are getting the social media and user generated sites aiding and abetting the mainstream western media view of this as a massive liberal explosion in Iran.[22]

The BBC's coverage of the Iranian election shows that the population who use social media shapes them. Other research has also found that during the election, journalists turned to traditional sources including political statements, expert opinions, and the "man on the street" to add colour to reportage with their quotes (Knight, 2012). A similar phenomenon took place during the Haiti earthquake in 2010. At the beginning of the coverage of the earthquake, Carel Pedre, a Haitian radio host, and Troy Livesay, a U.S. Christian missionary working in the country's capital, Port-au-Prince, were the main tweeters journalists used as direct sources. BBC journalists must follow the BBC Editorial Guidelines when reporting events. For instance, the guidelines highlight that when developing contacts on social media, journalists should be careful. According to the BBC Editorial Guidelines, "you may wish to make 'friends' on a third party web page. Remember that approving a 'friend' may make other users of a site think they are more trustworthy" (BBC, 2011). The guidelines also recommend that before approving friends, journalists check their profile and ask a senior editorial figure for advice. The guidelines ask journalists to review friends and remove them if they exceed a threshold. Journalists thus face several constraints when they use social media, including abiding by the editorial guidelines. Social media bring a new set of questions and create new spaces of communication online. Several important news events demonstrate how journalists' uses of social media have become much more sophisticated in the ensuing years, and that journalists took the opportunity to bolster their traditional norms and practices in crisis reporting. At the same time, reporting was becoming increasingly collaborative.

THE NEW EDITOR'S JOB: FORMALISING SOCIAL MEDIA

At the end of 2009, senior managers were looking at social media "both in terms of guidelines and controls, but equally the opportunities because we can see there are so many people who are interested in consuming social media in a shared social space: debating it, sharing and so forth", said Director General Mark Thompson (cited in Townend, 2009). Journalists "still got to think very hard about the reputation of the BBC and its journalism even if it's not in the context of a BBC service", added Thompson (cited in Townend, 2009). Indeed,

> If you look very closely at what we do: they're some things called blogs. Robert Peston on the web and [his] web reports, those are balanced pieces of journalism . . . It may be in the form of a blog but it's carefully balanced—it's checked by a senior editorial manager, it's fact-checked. It's a piece of essentially broadcast journalism.
>
> (Thompson cited in Townend, 2009)

In November 2009, a few months after the presidential election in Iran, the BBC created a Social Media Editor position. This initiative represented a significant step in the BBC's efforts to centrally manage social media. Mary Hockaday, the BBC's Head of Newsroom, said that the new Social Media Editor position would "help develop new ways for audiences to have their say on stories being covered by BBC News, and to ensure technology was developed to support the social media and UGC operations across BBC Journalism" (Hockaday quoted in BBC, 2009). The new Editor would "coordinate the work of correspondents and reporters using social media tools, ensuring that best practice was developed and shared within BBC Journalism" and "manage the existing UGC Hub within BBC Newswire, coordinating high-quality UGC news gathering and effective comment and debate on all of the Newsroom platforms", Hockaday added (BBC, 2009). Newswire was launched prior to Alex Gubbay's appointment in 2008 as part of the BBC's Delivering Creative Future plan that centralised the production team (BBC, 2009).

Alex Gubbay was the first Social Media Editor at the BBC. Before becoming Social Media Editor, Gubbay was Interactive Sports News Editor for BBC Sport, a unit that has developed several innovations in social media newsgathering. Gubbay served from 2009 until early 2011. That year, Chris Hamilton took over his role. Gubbay's appointment was an important decision: Social media were becoming increasingly valuable in BBC journalism and Alex Gubbay had acquired professional experience that would help him lead the BBC's social media efforts throughout the achievement of the next stage. This move by senior management shows that social media were gradually integrated in the daily activities of BBC journalists, and that the BBC created new strategic positions involving techies in the newsroom because of the need to manage social media material.

THE HAITI EARTHQUAKE: THE POWER OF CROWDSOURCING

On 12 January 2010, a powerful earthquake devastated Haiti. This time, the BBC had a set of guidelines and a Social Media Editor, and was prepared to make social media a major component of its reporting. Journalists perceived the earthquake as a news event that provided the BBC with social media experiences and helped enhance its public broadcasting value. The BBC covered the event by combining tweets from the area with coverage by its reporter in Port-au-Prince. The BBC website encouraged readers to e-mail pictures to yourpics@bbc.co.uk upload videos, and follow the organisation on BBC_HaveYourSay/haiti, the Twitter account @BBC_HaveYourSay, and the Twitter hashtag #haiti.

The U.S. Geological Survey Department first broke the news of the earthquake. The Department declared that a quake of 7.3 on the Richter scale hit Haiti at 4:53 p.m. local time. No more information was available to BBC journalists because none were at the site of the events.[23] An Associated Press American correspondent was the only full-time mainstream news reporter posted on the scene of the tremors. The Associated Press journalist was one of the main sources of information, but local stringers also provided eyewitness accounts of the events. Haiti Reuters correspondent Joseph Guyler Delva related: "everything started shaking, people were screaming, houses started collapsing" (Delva quoted in BBC, 2010c). Delva added, "I saw people under the rubble, and people killed. People were screaming 'Jesus, Jesus' and running in all directions" (Delva quoted in BBC, 2010c). Henry Bahn, an official for the U.S. Agriculture Department visiting Haiti that day, said that everyone in Haiti was "just totally freaked out and shaken" (Bahn quoted in BBC, 2010c).

Due to a lack of access to journalistic accounts at the time the quake occurred, the BBC sought user-generated content on social media platforms. According to Eltringham, Twitter "provided an absolutely essential gateway to reporting the Haiti earthquake" (Eltringham, 2010). Eltringham elaborated:

> Tweeters and the information they Tweeted proved reliable and, as the Web was the only means of communication that survived the disaster, crucial in sustaining coverage of the story until conventional journalism was able to mobilise 24 hours or more later.
>
> (Eltringham, 2010)

Haitians started tweeting. Twitter was one of the only sources of information that journalists had access to. In the first 24 hours after the earthquake, social media became the most relevant source of information for journalists trying to report the crisis (Eltringham, 2010). Twitter had thus played a significant role in distributing early information to news organisations about the quake. Reflecting this idea, Matthew Eltringham of the BBC User-Generated Content Hub wrote,

> Within a few hours of the earthquake, the UGC Hub sourced key— and unique—testimony from Tweeters in Haiti, like @carelpedre and

@troylivesay. These two in particular used Twitter to report rapidly and accurately about the situation on the ground in the earthquake zone and became significant voices throughout the course of the story. Ushahidi used Twitter to help build a crowd-sourced map to direct the aid effort. Others were using Twitter to point journalists to sources of further information.

(Eltringham, 2010)

For example, Haitian photographer Fredoux Dupoux posted the first tweet at 5 p.m. local time. He wrote, "Oh shiet [sic] heavy earthquake right now in Haiti". Subsequently, @FutureHaiti tweeted, "Earthquake 7 Richter scale just happening #Haiti" (MacLeod, 2010). On Twitter, the BBC communicated mainly with two people: the radio host Carel Pedre and the missionary Troy Livesay. Pedre tweeted at 7 p.m., approximately two hours after the earthquake, "if you need To get in Touch with friend and family in Haiti. Send me a Private Message with names and phone numbers. I'll get Back to U!". Later on, Pedre wrote, "For All My International Medias, Check out the last pics I took @Petion-Ville here http://bit.ly/7YQusz".

In contrast, Livesay sent descriptive and emotional tweets, including: "Church groups are singing throughout the city all through the night in prayer. It is a beautiful sound in the middle of a horrible tragedy". Both tweeters helped BBC journalists produce news pieces on the shocks, each adding their own value. James Morgan, a BBC broadcast journalist, recalls,

I definitely remember we didn't have much information and we were on Twitter looking for news coming from Haiti. I remember we found someone (Pedre) who was tweeting from Haiti and was able to talk, telling us something we could transcribe for our website.

(Morgan quoted in Bruno, 2011)

Likewise, Matthew Eltringham (2010) elevated Twitter as a reliable source of information in crisis reporting: "Tweeters and the information they Tweeted proved reliable and, as the Web was the only means of communication that survived the disaster, crucial in sustaining coverage of the story until conventional journalism was able to mobilise 24 hours or more later" (Eltringham, 2010). Found by a BBC UGC Hub journalist as a source on Twitter, Pedre provided images and testimonies for the BBC. For instance, the BBC World Service Radio and TV produced an interview through Skype with Pedre. This interview was possible because of the generator at Pedre's Haitian radio station (MacLeod, 2010).

Skype was also a useful tool for journalists to access sources. Pierre Cote, a Haitian journalist, conducted an interview with BBC News using Skype, speaking about his role as a Haitian who communicated with the outside world about the quake and its aftermath (Palmer, 2010). The Today Programme on radio broadcasted the interview with Cote. The host of the BBC radio programme and Pedre discussed the physical environment in Haiti and the extent of the damages brought by the earthquake. Pedre said, "I saw a lot of people crying for help, a lot of buildings collapsed, a lot of car damage, a lot of people without help, people bleeding" (BBC, 2010c). Google and Facebook also provided missing people lists. Journalists used the Twitter hashtag #relativesinhaiti to find Haitian loved ones and #rescumehaiti to direct rescue efforts of trapped persons. For example, the BBC journalist Lewis MacLeod described how the earthquake damaged other means of communication, leaving social media the most useful option for reporters:

> Traditional news media, such as national TV channels and newspapers, accepted the mass of material as vital in delivering the story in its early stages in the context of a severely damaged communications and transport infrastructure, chronic power failure, and extensive damage to key buildings in the capital.
>
> (MacLeod, 2010)

Journalists also used crowdsourcing, which refers to when "tasks traditionally performed by employees are outsourced to a large network of people, recruited through an open call" (Muthukumaraswamy, 2010, 48). Jeff Howe, Editor of the U.S. magazine *Wired*, coined the term as "the act of taking a job traditionally performed by a designated agent [usually an employee] and outsourcing it to an undefined generally large group of people in the form of an open call" (Howe, 2006). Besides using Twitter as a newsgathering tool, journalists used the crowdsourcing map Ushahidi, which refers to "witness" in Swahili, to aggregate information. The open-source Ushahidi provided map details of damaged areas and aid-distribution efforts (BBC, 2010). The mapping tool was first developed during the Kenyan election in 2007 and utilised SMS and Google Earth to cover the post-election violence in different parts of the country. During the Haiti earthquake in 2010, Ushahidi used a dynamic map that brought together updates from blog posts, e-mails, Google, SMS messages, tweets, and other user-generated content sources such as uploaded audio, pictures, texts, and videos (Cooper, 2011). Using SMS and Google Earth, Ushahidi showed natural hazards, services available, security threats, health risks, and infrastructure damage. The website had a section where users could follow and verify Twitter accounts, tag photos, and monitor citizen journalism and mainstream news.

Patrick Meier, from the Harvard Humanitarian Initiative (HHI),[24] helped Ushahidi to raise funds from the U.S. government. During the quake, Meier asked for help through his network. This effort resulted in around 300 students from Tufts University volunteering to manage the flow of information from individuals who reported damage or missing persons (Cooper, 2011, 21). The open-source website operators made an agreement with Digicel, a Haitian mobile phone operator, creating a short-code to which users texted messages about the unfolding events. Ushahidi also set up "situation rooms" in Boston, Washington, and Geneva, and more than 10,000 Haitians volunteered to translate messages from Creole to English and communicate with Creole speakers. Organisations and individuals in Haiti were able to use the information provided on Ushahidi to find areas of crisis and direct rescue efforts. According to Eltringham, "Ushahidi used Twitter to help build a crowdsourced map to direct the aid effort. Others were using Twitter to point journalists to sources for further information" (Eltringham, 2010).

Journalists at the BBC quickly realised the value of the information that they found on social media. In interviews, journalists said that they were eager to reach Twitter-based sources in addition to the voices of their journalism. A new media logic was developing, involving a greater collaboration between BBC journalists and audiences. Communication scholar Lillie Chouliaraki recalls that in news coverage of the 2008 Mumbai attacks, journalists put their voices next to those of citizens witnessing the events by placing the pronoun "I" of the professional next to the citizen on the live feed: "23.09 The BBC's Andy Gallacher says:[25] 'I've just arrived at Port-au-Prince and aid is now coming in, but very slowly indeed. There are just a few US Coast Guard and a few military planes here'" (Chouliaraki, 2010, 315). Chouliaraki argues that "insofar as such structural changes result in replacing the logic of news as storytelling with a logic of news as techno-textual interactivity . . . post-television witnessing of events can be seen as becoming increasingly technologized. . . . It has enabled the emergence of ordinary witnessing and the manifestation of a caring ethos towards vulnerable others" (Chouliaraki, 2010, 319). Building on old journalistic practices of verification, on the day of the initial earthquake, Morgan wrote to Pedre: "Hi! It's James here, the BBC News. We saw your tweets in Haiti and we'd like to talk to you. Please, can you send us a message back?" (Morgan quoted in Bruno, 2011). Pedre replied to Morgan and thus began a process of authentication, with the radio host using standard BBC verification practices. These included talking to Pedre, asking what he saw around him, checking his IP address and phone number prefix to confirm his location, Googling him, and looking at his Twitter followers to establish credibility. Through these steps, Morgan verified social media content through the principle of accuracy.

It is important to note that despite news organisations' enthusiasm for journalistic uses of social media in crisis reporting, research has shown that social media have not replaced traditional reporting, but have instead become part of the process. At the Reuters Institute for the Study of Journalism at Oxford University, Nicola Bruno (2011) conducted content analysis of the social media impact on the coverage of the Haiti earthquake, for example. In this research, Bruno suggested that social media at the BBC was only part of the reporting:

> During the entire day of 13 January the website reposted audio contributions from non-governmental organisations, in various formats and

contexts—a clear sign that the BBC considered these sources more reliable and valuable. In fact, more than half of the reporting that day (52%) was based on GN sources [government agencies, non-governmental organisations, public officials, scientific community experts]. . . . 13% (40 items) was reserved to UGC—as mentioned earlier, mostly Carel Pedre's material and several tweets by Troy Livesay ('Tweets from @ troylivesay spoke of the worst damage being in the Carrefour district, where 'many two and three storey buildings did not make it')'. In very few instances, the BBC website published his tweets with a disclaimer not at the bottom of its more general stories: 'Reports on the Twitter message site, which cannot yet be verified by the BBC, expressed the chaos in the wake of the quake'.

(Bruno, 2011)

Journalists' uses of social media during the earthquake demonstrate that crowdsourcing does not replace traditional journalistic practices. Rather, journalists still select, curate, and choose if and how they use social media. In the case of the 2010 Haiti earthquake, journalists processed most social media activities through the UGC Hub, as crowdsourcing emerged as a new journalistic practice. This example of crowdsourcing as a new object and practice shows an important interrelation with an old object that journalists take into account when they use social media—that is, the BBC's editorial expectations. These expectations are published in the Editorial Guidelines and social media guidance. These editorial expectations indicate to BBC journalists the code of conduct that they must follow when producing the news.

Building on the BBC's experience with the Haiti earthquake, in May 2010 the BBC published an updated set of guidelines. The updated guidance indicated that social media were more about a conversation with than control of the news organisation by recommending reporters to follow a list of practices:

- Participate online; don't "broadcast" messages to users.
- Don't bring the BBC into disrepute.
- With moderation, only police where we have to.
- Trust our users.
- Be open and transparent in our social media dealings.
- Consider the risk that "re-tweeting" of third party content by the BBC may appear to be an endorsement of the original author's point of view.
- Add your own comment to the "tweet" you have selected, making it clear why you are forwarding it and where you are speaking in your own voice and where you are quoting someone else's.

(Editorial Guidelines, 2009)

Authentication of news sources began long before the BBC guidelines were written and institutionalised in news production. Morgan authenticated the

Haitian radio host's statements through a series of questions. Due accuracy and due impartiality were important journalistic considerations. The UGC Hub journalist's verification of the Haitian tweeter fits within the guidance. In BBC news production, there is a set of tensions and negotiations among objects, leading to new journalistic practices, including crowdsourcing.

What followed revealed the changing relationship between the BBC and its audience. In 2010, Peter Horrocks, BBC World Service Director, gave a keynote address to BBC staff to celebrate the launch of the College of Journalism and BBC Global News Creative Network's Fit for the Future season. Horrocks spoke about the urgency for journalists to engage with social media at an organisational and personal level. In that speech, Horrocks made clear the importance he placed on social media as a tool for reporters:[26]

> Today, if you haven't got Twitter feeds set up to follow particular journalists and experts, if you're not making the most of Twitter lists, Google [Buzz] or net readers for RSS feeds. If you're not taking an active part in the world of social media and using the technologies available at your fingertips, then you're not doing your job, because your competitor is.[27]

Horrocks's above speech excerpt signals that after a period of adaptation, senior managers conceived social media as a major part of the BBC's newsgathering. By the end of 2010, senior managers stated that social media had become indispensable. For example, Horrocks stated to journalists, "Tweet or be sacked!". He added, "this isn't just a kind of fad from someone who's an enthusiast of technology. I'm afraid you're not doing your job if you can't do those things. It's not discretionary" (Horrocks cited in Bunz, 2010). He added that if journalists did not like it, they should be doing something else. Institutionalised in corporate speech, social media were portrayed as a necessary part of news production for BBC senior managers, and a handful of journalists who had taken the leading role in shaping social media in the Corporation.

SOCIAL MEDIA ARE NOT DISCRETIONARY ANYMORE!

After the Haiti earthquake in 2010, social media were partly integrated in BBC journalism. Although senior management pushed staff to take the leap, there was still some resistance from journalists. BBC reporters far from universally accepted social media in their journalism. On the one hand, some journalists were wary of limitations in their reporting and understood the necessity to engage with social media to improve it. On the other hand, "the majority of journalists understand social media offers a range of new tools for newsgathering and building community, but understand it should be treated with caution, and the subtleties appreciated" (Wardle, 2010).

Journalists such as Lyse Doucet, BBC Chief International Correspondent, said that many BBC reporters remained skeptical "for a year after Horrocks' speech" (Doucet, 2011). The Arab Spring helped change her perspective, Doucet added. While covering the events in Tunisia, the correspondent, like many of her colleagues at the BBC, used social media tactics she had learned during previous coverage at the BBC.[28] The integration of social media in BBC journalism was thus not a simple linear process of technological adoption in the newsroom. Rather, it was—and remains—the result of new information technologies ushered in by the UGC Hub, social media trainers, senior managers, and a selection of influential journalists.

Crisis reporting has provided an opportunity for BBC journalists to reinforce norms such as impartiality, by developing and highlighting a set of old and new practices and norms. Different mechanisms facilitated the integration period through the series of news events discussed above. These mechanisms included the BBC's launch of its social networking guidelines in 2008, the publication of the social media guidelines in 2010, the development of verification techniques to prevent hoaxes and inaccuracies in reporting, speeches by senior managers promoting social media within the BBC, the establishment of a new Social Media Editor, and the move of the UGC to the heart of the newsroom. These cases allowed for a new order involving citizen witnessing through social media in BBC crisis reporting.

NOTES

1. UGC Hub Manager, interview 2012.
2. 24/7 News Editor, interview 2011.
3. World News Editor, interview 2011.
4. World News Editor, interview 2011.
5. World News Editor, interview 2011.
6. The Media Society is a charity organization hosting events on media in the United Kingdom.
7. An earlier version of this section can be found in Belair-Gagnon, V. (2013) 'Revisiting Impartiality: Social Media and Journalism at the BBC', *Symbolic Interaction*, 36(4): 478–492.
8. See: http://www.flickr.com/photos/vinu.
9. See: http://mumbai.metblogs.com/2008/11/10/the-mumbai-laundry.
10. Shortly after the release of the Neil Report, in 2005, Michael Grade, Chairperson of the BBC Board of Governors, delivered the "Goodman Media Lecture" discussing the future of impartiality and the challenges it faced from new technologies. He asked, "Do we have a really robust understanding of what it means for the BBC in the 21st Century? Of what it would mean if we were left standing as the only broadcaster still committed to delivering an impartial news service"? Following this speech, the BBC Trust published a report entitled *From Seesaw to Wagon Wheel: Safeguarding Impartiality in the 21st Century* (BBC, 2007). The report states that Grade's speech prompted the BBC's reflection on impartiality. But the report's publication was embedded in a wider corporate and information technology context: General Manager Mark Thompson responded to the publication of the 2006 White Paper by

unveiling Creative Future and the "Martini media" approach, referring to BBC on demand—anytime, anyplace, anywhere. This approach promoting "the 'fewer, bigger, better' formula adopted at the BBC as part of its restructuring to a multimedia entity clearly acknowledges that breadth must suffer to support more innovative and potentially high-impact content proposals" (Doyle, 2010, 15). According to Kevin Marsh (2010), *From Seesaw to Wagon Wheel* was significant for BBC journalism; it signalled that the previous conception of impartiality as bipolar idea (seesaw) had been replaced with multiple axes (wagon wheel). The report eventually became the foundation for teaching at the College of Journalism for the Corporation's 7,500 journalists, including the social media courses. The report argued that the BBC should take more serious action to protect impartiality in a new media environment. *From Seesaw to Wagon Wheel* also targeted the Internet as a potential disruptor of BBC impartiality: "Properly handled, UGC is an important new resource for news programmes. UGC, which is not directly offered to the BBC but is circulating on the web poses additional problems. It may be impossible to identify (let alone speak to) the source, and such material should be handled with caution" (BBC, 2007, 80). It predicted that user-generated content would become journalistic sources, and that this information would be processed and centralised in the UGC Hub operations. The way social media were handled by "impartial" journalists in times of crisis reflects the "collaborative journalism" trend of the period. At the same time, crisis reporting has provided an opportunity for BBC journalists to reinforce impartiality by developing and highlighting a set of new values and practices bolstered by old ones.

11. In 1926, the conservative government of Stanley Baldwin governed Britain. Baldwin was in office from 23 May 1923 to 16 January 1924, and from 4 November 1924 to 5 June 1929. At the time, the coal industry had been strongly hit by the rising value of the pound sterling, which had increased the price of exports. One of the ways that coal producers saw they could reduce the price of exports was by cutting wages and increasing the hours of work of the coal miners. With negotiations at a deadlock, on 4 May 1926, the Trade Union Congress (TUC) called a general strike. The TUC asked the UK government to maintain wages and alleviate the worsening conditions faced by coal miners. John Reith, the first General Manager of the BBC, agreed with Baldwin that the strike could undermine the government and therefore should be stopped. Reith also saw the strike as an opportunity to demonstrate what the BBC could do in times of crises. During the strike, Reith appealed for BBC independence to Winston Churchill, who wanted the BBC to support the government. In a series of exchanges with Baldwin, Reith said that having the government tell the BBC what to do would weaken the Corporation's reputation of independence and impartiality. Baldwin responded favourably to Reith's request. Churchill "emphatically objected and said it was monstrous not to use such an instrument to the best possible advantage" (Briggs, 1995, 332). After much debate, Baldwin's cabinet decided not to commandeer the BBC during the strike (Briggs, 1995, 333). Although Reith said that the BBC reported the events with a sense of impartiality, he allowed reporting from TUC and refused to air comments from the Archbishop of Canterbury, who insisted on an end to the strike. More controversially, Reith helped Prime Minister Baldwin write a speech to the nation that he delivered from Reith's home in Westminster. During the strike, the BBC interpreted impartiality through a particular moral and political lens, with Reith supporting the government (Curran and Seaton, 2003, 114). "Reith articulated the BBC position in those words: 'Assuming the BBC is for the people, and that the government is for

the people, then the BBC must be for the government in this crisis'" (Williams, 1998, 100). In his diary, Reith noted that "[t]hey want to be able to say that they did not commandeer us, but they know they can trust us not to be really impartial" (Stuart, 1975, 96). Although the BBC has vigorously denied that it has yielded to the UK government pressures, researchers have found evidence in the BBC archives demonstrating otherwise. Peter Ayton and Howard Tumber discovered that: "perception ives bias of the BBC bias is a complex phenomenon that seems to be influenced by journalism, psychology and the nature of the relationship real and imagined—between broadcaster and politics" (Ayton and Tumber, 2001, 13). Immediately after the strike, Reith wrote a letter to the head of department, station directors, and superintendent engineers. In this confidential letter, Reith discussed his dilemma during the strike. He demonstrated the desire of the BBC to produce "authentic impartial news" and be "an organisation within the constitution" (Briggs, 1995, 334). The BBC emerged from the strike with an ethic of political neutrality, eventually leading the Corporation to state that a government intervention was its own decision (Curran and Seaton, 2003, 119). In the meantime, on 5 March 1926, the Crawford Committee recommended that the BBC broadcast a "moderate amount of controversial matter" (Briggs, 1961, 352). The government accepted this recommendation on 14 July 1926. Reith's lobbying during the strike was successful. On 15 November 1926, during the debate on the BBC's new charter, Lord Wolmer, the assistant Postmaster General, reported, "I want to make this service not a Department of State, and still less the creature of the Executive, but as far as is consistent with ministerial responsibility, I wish to create an independent body of trustees operating the service in the interests of the public as a whole" (Wolmer in Briggs, 1961, 360). The strike was an opportunity for Reith to highlight in a moment of national crisis important concepts defining the BBC, including impartiality, balance, and independence. At this time, Reith's concept of impartiality remained only partly developed in practice.

12. Refer to: http://blogs.journalism.co.uk/2008/12/04/mumbai-and-twitter-how-the-bbc-dealt-with-tweets-and-accuracy/ and http://www.theguardian.com/media/pda/2008/dec/05/bbc-twitter.
13. Female foreign correspondent, interview 2011.
14. Female foreign correspondent, interview 2011.
15. Editor, interview 2011.
16. From 1926 to 2007 the main governing body of the BBC was the Board of Governors. On 1 January 2007, the BBC Trust replaced the Board. Similar to the BBC Board of Governors, the Trust operates independently from the Executive Board led by the Director General. The Trust acts as the in-house transparent body responsible for evaluating the performance of the BBC and advocating for the BBC and the interests of the licence fee-paying public. The duties of the Trust correlate with those of the regulator Ofcom. In contrast with Ofcom, the role of the BBC Trust is to set out a framework for editorial and creative output while being held to account by the licence fee payers. The creation of the Trust cemented the principle that the BBC operates at arm's length from government interests. Institutional bodies such as the Board of Governors (until 2007) and the BBC Trust (since 2007) have sought to safeguard BBC independence by promoting quality journalism. For example, in practice, in 2011, the Trust acted as the "safeguard" of impartiality of the BBC coverage of the Arab Spring. The Trust released a report on the BBC coverage of the Arab Spring led by Edward Mortimer, former United Nations Director of Communications, expert in Middle East affairs, and former

Senior Vice President of the Salzburg Global Seminar, an independent and non-governmental organisation that acts as a platform to discuss global challenges such as global citizenship, institutional philanthropy, and reforms and transformation in the Middle East. Mortimer stated that the BBC coverage of the Arab Spring was satisfactory. He expressed concerns over the coverage, and the non-coverage, of certain events that occurred in the Middle East (BBC Trust, 2012). For example, the report stated that the BBC failed to explain the specific context of the Bahrain uprising: Sunnis constrained the Shias because of fears that if the Shias dominated Bahrain, the country would become an Iranian proxy. The report therefore recommended that the BBC have a greater range of sources and diversity of outputs.

17. Assistant Editor Social Media, interview 2011.
18. Six and 10 O'clock News Producer, interview 2011.
19. Six and 10 O'clock News Producer, interview 2011.
20. Six and 10 O'clock News Producer, interview 2011.
21. During the 2013 Iranian election, researchers noticed the media strategy of the programme Nobat e Shoma with Twitter handle @bbcshoma to actively tweet to people to ask them questions for the TV show. Evidence shows that they eventually became central in the conversation on Twitter, a factor they need to account for (see Hassanpour et al., 2014).
22. Today Programme interview quoted in Newman, 2009, 27.
23. Assistant Editor UGC Hub, interview 2011; Deployment staff, interview 2011.
24. Meier is founder of CrisisMappers Network, The Digital Humanitarian Network, and the 56Standby Ta67sk Force. He is now Director of Social Innovation at Qatar Computing Research Institute.
25. Lillie Chouliaraki emphasised these words in bold in her article.
26. This excerpt was taken from notes from the "Fit for the Future" speech provided to me by Horrocks's office.
27. The text in bold in the quote was highlighted by Peter Horrocks in his notes.
28. Lyse Doucet made a similar comment as the one mentioned above on a panel on the 2011 Arab Spring at the annual POLIS conference held at the London School of Economics on Friday, 23 March 2012.

3 A New Order

I have sat in meetings where people have been saying, 'it's the age of user-generated content'. Have they read local newspapers? 90% of it is generated by the public and written by staff. It's been going on like that for a hundred years. User-Generated Content is not new, the delivery is. 'Candid Camera' . . . or 'You Have Been Framed' is user-generated content. Quite commonly people who are unaware of the history of the industry will proclaim it as new when it is actually in very recognisable form in previous ways.

(BBC Wales Online News Editor, interview 2011)

THE CONSOLIDATION OF SOCIAL MEDIA

At the 2011 International Broadcasting Convention in Amsterdam, Kevin Bakhurst, former Deputy Head of the BBC newsroom, gave a speech discussing three ways social media have contributed to the transformation of the newsroom's work. The first was in newsgathering. He stated that social media "helps us gather more, and sometimes better, material; we can find a wider ranges of voices, ideas and eyewitnesses quickly". The second was in audience engagement. According to Bakhurst, the UGC Hub allowed the BBC to "fully engage in using this material, and reinforce the BBC values that our audience expects, in particular accuracy". Third, Bakhurst said that social media have become a platform for BBC content: "it's a way of us getting our journalism out there, in short form or as a tool to take people to our journalism on the website, TV or radio. It allows us to engage different and younger audiences". Bakhurst highlighted the mixture of opportunities and constraints that develops when journalists employ social media in news organisational contexts. For instance, social media present an opportunity for the BBC in terms of newsgathering, news distribution, and collaboration with audiences via social media. A question remains: How is this senior manager's speech reflected in the BBC's contemporary crisis reporting?

The BBC's uses of social media have been developed during a succession of major breaking news stories. Each of those stories has inspired new uses and prompted new questions. This chapter elaborates on changes in journalism by shifting attention to social media at the BBC since 2011. It reflects on how journalists used social media in the Tunisian uprisings during the "Arab Spring" and the death of Osama bin Laden in 2011. This chapter also looks at the emergence of new structures in the newsroom, with an emphasis on training and new editorial guidelines. The last section of this chapter draws from interviews with foreign correspondents and explores how journalists came to use social media as a source of information.

With the arrival of social media as a journalistic tool, BBC journalists found new ways to perform old tasks. At the same time, social media have become part of newsgathering. Photographs and videos created by citizens have become common features in mainstream news coverage. User-generated content is "approached as a potential force of change that transforms professional imageries of journalism vis-à-vis crisis events" (Anden-Papadopoulos and Pantti, 2013). Although "journalists' boundary work is at its fiercest in the domain of their perceived expertise", journalists feel pressured to adapt to the amateur media culture and citizen imageries resulting in an emerging logic of open participation, transparency, and amateurism in the networked media culture (Anden-Papadopoulos and Pantti, 2013, 973–974).

The emergence of new spaces of communication in both news input and output allows BBC audiences to participate in BBC's journalism by providing content in crisis reporting. Today, audiences are more involved in the dissemination of news. As the upshot of socio-technological and politico-economic changes occurring at the BBC and the media industry, from 2011 onward journalists have made social media a part of their reporting toolkit. The struggle to understand and manage social media in BBC journalism should be interpreted in the context of crisis news reporting, journalistic conventions, and the BBC in a period of political, economic, cultural, and institutional shift. Although limited to the BBC in the context of crisis reporting, the news production practices and norms of public broadcasting are similar to those of like-minded broadcasters.

THE TUNISIAN UPRISINGS

The first days of the 2011 Tunisian uprisings show that the BBC recognised the potential for social media in crisis news production. On 12 January 2011, after clashes between the police and protesters, the Tunisian government established a curfew in Tunis and surrounding regions. As a result, reporting in the streets was dangerous for journalists. Lyse Doucet, BBC Chief International Correspondent, was in Tunis that day. During the 9 a.m. BBC Television Centre newsroom editorial meeting, an editor mentioned that journalists in Tunis, including Doucet, could report the news only from their hotel while the city was under curfew. Doucet (2011) mentioned that she was able to gather eyewitness evidence in the streets of the

Tunisian capital. During the editorial meeting, the editor prevented news teams from sending additional reporters to Tunis until he had given his consent. He provided two main reasons for this decision. First, the curfew limited journalists' ability to report from the streets of Tunis. Second, the uprising could compromise the safety of journalists. As in other crisis news reporting events explored in this book, journalists faced major challenges in finding eyewitness accounts to report a significant news story. These events provided journalists with ideal opportunities to use social media in their work. At the same time, the BBC strived to retain its authority as a public broadcaster of news.[1]

The events surrounding the uprisings provided challenges for journalists in terms of newsgathering. Each uprising in the Middle East and North Africa had its own internal social media operation. Lyse Doucet (2011) recalls how she used each social media platform during the uprising. In Tunisia, the revolution emerged in small towns and made its way to the capital thanks to political activists in the country using Facebook. The phenomenon in Egypt was more urban and gained strong followings in cities such as Alexandria, Suez, and Cairo. The epicentre of the revolution was Cairo's Tahrir Square; there, groups of young activists played a prominent role, coordinating via Twitter and Facebook, and using the square as a physical rallying point. In Damascus, Doucet relied on activist videos. In the BBC newsroom in London, where I was located at the time, social media were a central consideration.

During these events, Matthew Eltringham and a few other journalists started using social media platforms, including Twitter, with other organisations and individuals disseminating the news. Although they used social media, these tech-savvy journalists also started to resist certain features of social media (Anden-Papadopoulos and Pantti, 2013). One of the BBC's tactics was to divide the good from the not-so-good journalism using the idea of "the light side and the dark side of the verification line". This expression appeared in a blog post by the Editor of BBC College of Journalism, Matthew Eltringham, and Charlie Beckett, Director of POLIS,[2] on the BBC College of Journalism website. In first an informal conversation and second via the BBC College of Journalism, Eltringham and Beckett wanted to reconcile journalism with social media. For Eltringham, social media were a new technology that "often threatened to swamp newsgathering during big stories" (Eltringham, 2011c). In the BBC blog post, Eltringham and Beckett reflected on the idea of a line of verification.

In the past, Beckett wrote, BBC journalists would strive to broadcast only what was on the light side of verification: the truth, determined by a rigorous process of checking facts. According to the two journalists, this line of verification is part of the process of truth-telling journalism that the BBC strives to produce. In social media contexts, journalists must deal with the dark side of verification. "The question for the BBC and other news organizations is how to engage with the wealth of publicly available but unsubstantiated material on the 'Dark Side' of the line of verification while maintaining their journalistic standards" (Harkin et al., 2012, 11). For the BBC, individual pieces of journalism on the dark side of the line should be distrusted, whereas the BBC creates alliances with journalists on the light side.

Several mechanisms help the BBC remain on the light side of the verification line. For example, since the emergence of social media, the BBC has developed institutional infrastructure enabling BBC journalists to remain on the light side. Eltringham says that methods have enabled BBC journalists to separate non-journalistic sources from journalistic sources. Non-journalistic sources include e-mails, texts, tweets, blogs, and Facebook (Eltringham, 2011c). UGC Hub journalists process a vast array of online voices and develop methods to prevent mistakes. These methods include: verifying forensically before publishing, labelling, and contextualising.

The BBC has also developed other methods to bolster its journalism. BBC journalists have also taken part in training sessions held by the BBC Academy and College of Journalism to develop skills in processing social media content. Emma Meese, former Social Media Producer for BBC Wales News and Current Affairs, says that in training sessions, social media specialists instruct journalists to use citizen material "as news wire and contact book" (Meese quoted in Philips, 2012). A growing number of curators are also developing tools to select social media, allowing the organisation and its news output to remain on the light side of verification.

During the Russian elections in 2012, BBC World Service Future Media and the UK political social media Tweetminster developed a platform to visualise live updates from Twitter. Anna Vissens (2012), Interactive Editor of BBC Russian Service, said that BBC journalists selected preapproved groups, keywords, shared uniform resource locators (URLs), and active users. Echoing Vissens's statement, Beckett says that the BBC has become a curator: "we become increasingly significant as a reference or clearing house, filtering fact from fiction" (Beckett quoted in Eltringham, 2011c). In these social practices, particularly in curating newsworthy information, the BBC is able to practice a higher level of quality journalism on the light side of the line of verification. The BBC acted as a clearinghouse of user-generated content.

For Eltringham and Beckett, the line of verification has the function of separating the BBC from the noise that journalists manage on social media. On the opposite side of the line of verification lies the dark side, where information has not yet been confirmed as true. BBC journalists also draw on information in that space to produce the news. By using a rigorous process to establish credibility and confirm the identity and location of participants, BBC journalists are able to mitigate the uncertainty of content on the dark side of the verification line. The fact that BBC journalists produce the news using material from both sides of the line indicates that the line is fuzzy and far from absolute. In this context, the BBC creates new practices to distinguish its journalism from the other online voices. A series of verification methods performed by the UGC Hub as curator help BBC journalists to remain on the light side of verification. These methods, although helpful, reflect the tensions in the BBC's changing journalism. The BBC now crosses traditional broadcasting boundaries of television and radio. Journalists report directly onto social media platforms and communicate with audiences without the BBC as intermediary. This practice creates a new narrative in the news by producing news in a collaborative fashion, with ordinary citizens online.[3]

A striking example of online curating occurred on Friday, 14 January 2011, during an interaction on Twitter between Andy Carvin, NPR Social Media Editor, and Matthew Eltringham, BBC College of Journalism Editor.[4] During the Arab uprisings, Carvin attempted to tell the stories through Twitter. "A 'human router,' as the blog TechCrunch calls him, Carvin has spent the past two months—except for during meals with his family and when putting his children to bed—tweeting news out about the Middle East" (Bell, 2011). Carvin says,

> My preference is always to tweet information that's been confirmed, but Twitter is also great at verifying and debunking things. I'll often re-tweet stuff that isn't confirmed but ask my followers to help me get more context. Volunteers have helped me find the exact location where videos have been recorded, translate them, recognize the accent or dialect, etc. When I saw a photo of a Libyan holding what looking like a very large anti-tank round, I asked people to help me figure out what it was, and about a dozen people started researching it. Ultimately, one of my followers, who happens to be in the U.S. armed forces, identified it as a Russian-made anti-aircraft round, and sent me all the specs regarding it. Many of my Twitter followers end up playing the roles of producers, researchers, fixers and the like.
>
> (Carvin quoted in Bell, 2011)

Carvin represents a new breed of journalists who crowdsource online by gathering "information from their audiences or tap[ping] into the expertise or experience of their audiences to verify information" (Harkin et al., 2012, 11). A striking example of the BBC as clearinghouse occurred during the Tunisian uprisings in early January 2011. Carvin observed on Twitter that

> Several tweets claimed that staff at Tunisia's TV7 had turned against President Ben Ali on air. It was unclear to what extent they had done so. Someone sent me a video clip purporting to show the incident, and I re-tweeted it at 15:54 with a request for assistance in translating it: 'Does this video show TV7 staff turning against Ben Ali? Pls translate http://youtube/SL_FOXjx50k'.[5]

Less than a minute later, Carvin tweeted a second video, asking his followers for translation: "Need translated summary of this video from TV7 as well: http://on.fb.me/gdWqnl".[6] One of Carvin's 70,000+ Twitter followers, Matthew Eltringham saw Carvin's tweet and immediately asked the BBC Monitoring team whether Carvin's tweet was true.[7] The team confirmed to the BBC journalist that the Tunisian station continued to broadcast the government's line. That fact conflicted with what Carvin had tweeted earlier.[8] Eltringham tweeted to Carvin: "BBC Monitoring say TV7 maintaining its editorial line after some staff voiced their anger live". Carvin subsequently re-tweeted this tweet, annotating it with his own previous tweet: "A protest, not a takeover".[9]

Within minutes, Twitter followers with the appropriate language knowledge translated the clip, Carvin used this translation to understand the story, and he accordingly sent an update tweet to those following him online. As a result, Carvin, Eltringham, and a network of physically dispersed tweeters went beyond the traditional broadcast role: They sought others' thoughts on posts, and used these contributions to enrich their "broadcasts". As Harkin et al. write, "One key difference between the BBC's and Carvin's techniques is that the BBC verifies information first before publishing it to its news website or to its Twitter streams, while Carvin posts things that require additional confirmation to Twitter and asks for help in verifying them" (2012, 12). In this case, the BBC performed public service journalism outside the traditional newsroom and forms of broadcasting on Twitter by developing a set of processes to find out what the truth was with information on social media. At the same time, Carvin said, "Twitter can act like a newsroom, where bits of information are debated, sorted out and reported".[10]

As a result of these changes in the organisation of the newsroom, BBC news started to become more collaborative with its audiences while at the same time striving to retain its authority as public broadcaster. In the Arab Spring, verification had become "more than just a handy guide for journalists. The whole point is that journalists must now engage with social media. It is absolutely the space for networked journalism" (Beckett, 2011). Eltringham wrote that "social media unleashes the capacity of people to publish and share rumour, lies, facts and factoids. We—as a trusted broadcaster [along with other journalists, of course]—become increasingly significant as a reference or clearing house, filtering fact from fiction" (Eltringham, 2011). BBC News used social media to bolster its journalistic value of accuracy and verification. Echoing this remark, Eltringham writes,

'Old media' journalists are being forced to engage with the rumour, gossip, facts and factoids being circulated in places like Twitter and Facebook; to look at them and work out whether they are 'true' or not before running with them. Mainstream media cannot do without social media and social media are learning to leverage its power over mainstream media. Ultimately, although the principles of 'good journalism' remain the same, the landscape in which it operates is changing dramatically. And that, I think, is to the good—bringing transparency and accountability to everyone's journalism.

(Eltringham, 2011)

Alex Murray, BBC broadcast journalist at the UGC Hub, suggested that throughout Tunisia, Egypt, Libya, and Syria verification had become more complicated as social media content became more sophisticated: "[A]t the UGC Hub in the BBC Newsroom in London, our process has become much more forensic in nature" (Murray, 2011). For example, reporters used BBC expertise to verify social media content, adding to the narrative of the story. Everything that the BBC receives on social media goes through an intricate verification process. Journalists examine social media content forensically and, when they decide to publish it, add context to help audiences understand the nature and significance of the content. Since the unverified tweet scandal of the 2008 Mumbai attacks, the BBC has learned its lesson. And since the London bombing attacks of 2005, social media have consolidated in BBC journalism. Several studies describe in detail the cases that have shaped the media representation of the events (see, for example, Cottle, 2011). From the London Television Centre newsroom, I noticed those interactions taking place increasingly online and the UGC Hub taking an active part in shaping these events.[11] Through a series of reporting events, we observe the ways that reporting has become a messy patchwork of old and new media practices and norms where journalists and citizens choose to participate. This results in a more participatory media exchange and in new forms of journalism in crisis reporting (Bruns, 2008; Hjorth and Kim, 2011).

NEW AND MORE TRAINING: SOCIAL MEDIA AS PART OF THE FURNITURE

One crucial way that the BBC has strived to retain its public broadcasting authority has been in training. Training has become an institutional priority with the recent creation of the BBC College of Journalism. In November 2009, the BBC developed its first social media course, called Making the Web Work for You. The course trained BBC journalists about social media, how to find content and case studies, and how to build online communities. The course lasted one full working day and involved 15 journalists following the class on their laptops together in the same room. "It dealt with Facebook, but it also introduced people to digital tools on the Internet and how to use Google advanced search. The course was about social media, but also it was about Internet tools for journalists and for producers".[12] "It was very important that they were actually learning on the Internet as we were going along".[13] During the Arab Spring, journalists realised the value of using social media in their daily work (Doucet, 2011). Post-Arab Spring, in 2011, an important change took place in BBC social media training. The BBC started providing further one-on-one training sessions and created a forum for BBC journalists, independent media producers, and social media organisations. On 19 and 20 May 2011, the BBC held its first "Social Media Summit", where participants discussed changes in journalistic innovations, values, norms, editorial standards, and practices.

THE DEATH OF OSAMA BIN LADEN

In addition to the events and organisational moments described above, the journalistic tensions surrounding the death of Osama bin Laden demonstrate how social media have become a growing part of news production. This event highlights a more collaborative journalism in crisis reporting by the volume of user-generated content in news production.

On 2 May 2011, BBC Technology reporter Rory Cellan-Jones turned on the radio at 7 a.m. Listening to the news that morning, Cellan-Jones heard that Osama bin Laden had been killed in Abbottabad, Pakistan. Because this event was highly newsworthy, he "immediately picked up the phone and tweeted this fact" (Cellan-Jones, 2011). Cellan-Jones tweeted the news, believing that he was bringing something new to his Twitter followers, but was surprised when he was "bombarded with messages saying this was now very old news" (Cellan-Jones, 2011). With the availability of social media "you have to be online all night to keep up with events", Cellan-Jones (2011) wrote. In this case, journalists employed social media as a monitoring tool, before Cellan-Jones turned on the radio and heard the news. This event also shows how the relationship between the BBC and its audiences is evolving.

By social media standards, the death of bin Laden was old news; in fact, it was a case of inadvertent live tweeting. The night before, at 1 a.m., Sohaib Athar (@ReallyVirtual), describing himself on Twitter as "an IT consultant taking a break from the rat-race by hiding in the mountains with his laptops", tweeted the presence of a helicopter above Abbottabad: "Helicopter hovering above Abbottabad at 1AM (is a rare event)". "Athar typically tweeted about his daily concerns, ranging from his family to views on technology, politics and coffee (he and his wife manage a café) in the hope that is musings would be appreciated by his 750 or so followers" (Allan, 2013, 2). On that day, he shared his "irritation with the helicopter's noisy intrusion when to his astonishment a sudden explosion cut through the night" (Allan, 2013, 2).

Because Athar was trying to concentrate on his work, he described his annoyance with the noise of the helicopter. "I guess Abbottabad is going to get as crowded as the Lahore that I left behind for some peace. *sigh*", he

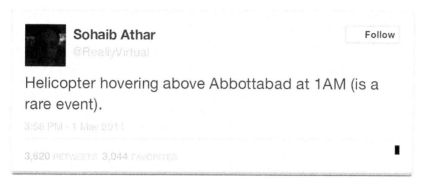

Sohaib Athar
@ReallyVirtual

Follow

Helicopter hovering above Abbottabad at 1AM (is a rare event).

3:58 PM - 1 May 2011

3,620 RETWEETS 3,044 FAVORITES

Figure 3.1   Sohaib Athar Tweet on Liveblogging bin Laden's Death

wrote on Twitter (Athar and Myers, 2012). Then Athar tweeted about an explosion, saying that something was going on in the town where he moved to have quiet and escape the tumult of city life. Shortly after, he tweeted, "Uh oh, now I'm the guy who live-blogged the Osama raid without knowing it". From the comfort of his home away from home, relaying information from his friends on Facebook, Athar had witnessed and chronicled the military raid that led to the death of bin Laden. Athar was not certain whether the information he gathered was true or not (Allan, 2013, 2). Twitter nevertheless enabled the IT consultant and café owner to disseminate this news to the rest of the world, albeit unintentionally.

Journalists recognised Athar as the first non-participant in the raid to witness the events unfolding in Pakistan on Twitter. Steve Myers,[14] Managing Editor of Poynter.org and who in 2012 hosted a panel with Athar at South By South West (SXSW), wrote,

> On his own, Athar couldn't distribute his observations very far. Indirectly, he did have access to a large network, though he probably didn't realize it at the time. He became influential because people in those networks recognized the importance of what he had observed and passed it on.
>
> (Athar and Myers, 2012)

Athar had 750 followers when he tweeted the news. The following Monday, he had accumulated 96,000 followers (Athar and Myers, 2012). Throughout the day after bin Laden's death, Athar was the key contact for mainstream news organisations covering the events. He posted pictures of news organisations setting up satellites dishes in Abbotabad. He also talked with the media (Athar and Myers, 2012).

A BBC journalist was the first reporter to reach Athar by telephone (Athar and Myers, 2012). The BBC journalist contacted him through a friend of a friend on Facebook. Athar did not know the journalist personally, but the journalist called the telephone number on Athar's personal Facebook page (Athar and Myers, 2012). Instead of signing exclusivity agreements with news organisations, Athar insisted on making his account of the events open online to all journalists and citizens. He used his blog to post a Q&A, which answered questions journalists asked him by e-mail and phone (Athar and Myers, 2012).

Former Defence Secretary Donald Rumsfeld's Chief of Staff Keith Urbahn was another influential node in the development of the story on Twitter. Urbahn tweeted at 10:25 p.m., "So I'm told by a reputable person they have killed Osama bin Laden. Hot damn".

Urbahn cautioned Twitter users against "getting ahead of the facts" (Allan, 2013, 3; Stelter, 2011) even after Athar tweeted the news: "Don't know if its true, but let's pray it is and Ladies, gents, let's wait to see what the President says. Could be misinformation or pure rumour". "Within minutes, anonymous sources at the Pentagon and the White House started to tell reporters the same information. ABC, CBS and NBC interrupted programming across the country at almost the same minute, 10:45 p.m., with the news", wrote Brian Stelter (2011), at the time a correspondent for *The New York Times*.

About an hour after Urbahn's tweet, at 11:35 p.m. Eastern Time, from Washington, DC, the White House (@whitehouse) tweeted, "President Obama: I can report to the American people and the world, that the U.S. has conducted an operation that killed Osama bin Laden". Then, before midnight, "Al Jazeera English network showed live pictures of a growing crowd outside the White House chanting 'USA! USA!'" (Stelter, 2011). Urbahn was not the first to disseminate the news, but he was the one who had the most trust on Twitter (Gilad Lothan, computer analyst, quoted in Allan, 2013, 3). Perhaps Urbahn was trusted to a greater extent than Athar had been earlier on the night of bin Laden's death.

@keithurbahn
Keith Urbahn

So I'm told by a reputable person they have killed Osama Bin Laden. Hot damn.

14 hours ago via Twitter for BlackBerry®   ☆ Favorite ⊠ Undo Retweet ↩ Reply

Retweeted by MaRiOdaBrAiN and others

Figure 3.2   Keith Urbahn Twitter Feed

The White House ✔
@WhiteHouse

☼   +👤 Follow

President Obama: "I can report to the
American people and to the world, that the
US has conducted an operation that killed
Osama bin Laden"

↩ Reply   ↻ Retweet   ★ Favorite   ••• More

RETWEETS   FAVORITES
4,392   638

4:35 AM - 2 May 2011

Figure 3.3   The White House Twitter Feed

According to Matt Rosoff, Editorial Director for CITEworld, Twitter had its "CNN moment" (Rosoff in Allan, 2013, 4). As Stuart Allan (2013) points out, other people beg to differ. BBC journalists used a range of social media sources, including Twitter, Wikipedia (with the Osama bin Laden entry), and Google Maps showing the Abbottabad compound, to monitor the news (Cellan-Jones, 2011). Journalists at the BBC employed social media tools to monitor early news events and integrate these events as part of the news input. BBC journalists used social media as a wire service to get information about bin Laden's death on Twitter. Journalists used the social media management tool Hootsuite to follow Twitter (Cellan-Jones, 2011). Journalists also used social media as a monitoring tool by using hashtags. Prominent Twitter hashtags included: #presidentobama, #osamadead, #osamabinladen, #osama, #usama, #osamabinladendead, #september11, #osamabinladen, #waronterror, #alquaeda, #twintowers, and #afghanistan. BBC journalists also used social media as a source by contacting Athar first by Facebook message and second by telephone. Journalists built the news story out of information found on social media.

BBC journalists were able to cover the death of Osama bin Laden. Yet journalists faced several challenges trying to use social media. First, hubs of influence such as Athar affect the flow of information on social networks. Athar did not want to sign an exclusivity agreement; he preferred to keep information flowing freely on the Internet. As a result, journalists' uses of social media have been influenced not only by organisational structures, but also by the relationships newsmakers form with online sources of information. A few key individuals also acted as hubs of influence. This limited the range of information available to journalists on social media.

Social media had become increasingly part of BBC journalistic input, within a media logic that gives preeminence to certain voices and allows citizens to play a more active role as witnesses. As Lillie Chouliaraki wrote, "major news institutions, such as the BBC, have also appropriated citizen journalism in their own cosmopolitanizing vision" (Chouliaraki, 2010, 306). This tendency involved changes in power relations among news consumers and producers, the content reported, and the effects on how the story is delivered to the public.[15]

TWITTER AND NEW JOURNALISTIC GUIDELINES

While social media gained significance in the newsroom, journalistic guidelines also evolved. In July 2011, the BBC updated its social media guidelines with new declarations focused on Twitter. The guidelines indicated that any content on @BBCBreaking and BBC News page on Facebook should be checked by a second person before being disseminated to audiences. Chris Hamilton, BBC Social Media Editor, writes,

> We label the Twitter accounts of some presenters and correspondents as 'official'—and are also today publishing some specific guidance for them. This activity is regarded as BBC News output and tweets should normally be consistent with this, reflecting and focusing on areas relevant to the role or specialism, and avoiding personal interests or unrelated issues. A senior editor keeps an eye on tweets from these accounts after they're sent out.
>
> (Hamilton, 2011)

The guidelines included the impact of Twitter on BBC journalism since the Iranian election of 2009.

NEWSGATHERING AND SOURCE SELECTION

Newsgathering and source selection, two fundamental components of the news cycle, have been at the centre of changes at the BBC. The BBC Newsgathering unit is located at the heart of the BBC Television Centre newsroom and provides live coverage for all BBC outlets and programmes. Journalists are divided into specialist areas: culture, community affairs, education, health, home and legal affairs, royal coverage, as well as science and the environment. Correspondents in regions including Wales, Northern Ireland, Scotland, the Midlands, and North and West of England cover news stories from their respective regions. The Economic and Business unit also furnishes coverage for the Corporation. Its programming includes Wake Up to Money, the Financial World Tonight on radio, BBC Two's Working

Lunch, and World Business Report for BBC World. The BBC's international bureaux provides the news to World Service Radio and BBC World. A story can also appear on BBC UK, although it is more likely that an international news story will appear on the Ten O'clock News.[16]

In London, the World Affairs unit, located in Bush House and Television Centre, covers world events. BBC foreign correspondents cover news stories for all BBC outlets and programmes. Newsgathering is an important unit whose decisions have ramifications throughout the news organisation worldwide. The newsgathering process is an integral part of the daily news cycle. It enables us to highlight how journalists perceive and manage social media within the structure of the Corporation. BBC journalists use social media as a source in four main ways: background information, direct source of information, storyline, and sources, which are organised around a preestablished hierarchy of sources.

Social Media as a Background Source of Information

Journalists have always relied on different types of sources to put the news together. Some sources are indirect, which means that the source is not quoted directly in the news piece. These sources help journalists understand crucial elements of the story before putting it together. Indeed, journalists do not always directly quote social media sources; instead, they frequently use social media sources for background information to put their stories together. For example, BBC journalists use social media such as Wikipedia, Storify, blogs, viral videos or video-sharing sites, such as those that can be found on YouTube or DailyMotion, to gain background information on news stories. As an example, Franz Strasser, reporter and video journalist with BBC News in Washington, wrote on his website: "I use Storify to gather feedback on my stories, follow up on changes resulting from my reports and visualise a debate from a panel" (Strasser, 2012). In another example, a foreign correspondent used a YouTube animated clip featuring different characters of central bankers during an economic crisis. This clip enabled journalists in the bureau to make sense of events:

> I may not use it, but you know it is a very interesting way of sort of monitoring what people are doing in social media . . . One of the things that sprung up, I did not use it for work, but it caught our attention about American central bankers . . . I may not have used it for work, but I found it interesting for interpreting subjects that I cover in different formats of media.[17]

This quote from a foreign correspondent contradicts the findings of Lariscy et al. (2009). Their research found that business journalists made little use of social media to find story ideas or sources. In my fieldwork, another male foreign correspondent noted that "during the Haiti earthquake

I remember following a few Twitter feeds. They helped giving a picture of what was going on".[18] In another example, a World Affairs unit reporter and Producer reported:

> I do use Twitter, but not so much for finding guest but rather to keep up to date with the developing stories. But sometimes—because also the thing that we try to do is to try to keep it fresh, try to not use the same people too often. Obviously there are people you are going to speak to more often than other. But sometimes, you might think that you want to have a guest on healthcare in America—you look on Google. You are looking around. Of course you check the veracity of your sources—but you might come across a think-tank that we are not using—they might have some good credentials—you might find them by Googling the tight words—things like that.[19]

A Six O'clock News and Ten O'clock News Editor stated that "we are much more likely to use mobile phone footage than we would have been few years ago and we are much more likely to hear about some of the development through Twitter or social media".[20] In these examples, journalists organised social media around their own work by negotiating social media as a source of background information to build their packaged news pieces.

Social Media as a Direct Source

A source is direct when journalists access sources and then quote that source explicitly in their news piece. Journalists can use social media sites including Facebook, LinkedIn, and Twitter to keep in touch with groups and individuals, and to find ordinary citizens' eyewitness accounts, which can enrich breaking news stories. For example, a female foreign correspondent observed:

> I use it to get a hold on people. Freelance type people who are difficult to reach by ordinary means because you have to go to publishers and the publishers to the agent and have to find their agent. It takes a long time. So as if you have to find someone like a woman she was a trend in marketing but she worked for loads of different people all the time. So I found her on Facebook and I asked her are you the woman who does blahblahblah . . . if you are I really got to talk to you. And she wrote back. That was it.[21]

Journalists increasingly use social media to track people down, such as when the BBC journalist communicated by phone with Athar after bin Laden's death. A female foreign correspondent considered social media a faster way to gain access to some sources:

> The only times I use social media for my work is to track people down because people often respond very quickly if you email them

on Facebook or poke them whatever. I do have a Twitter account, but I don't Tweet. I just don't have the time to keep up the flow. If you are on air a lot it is quite difficult to tweet as well.[22]

In the same vein, another male foreign correspondent said, "I use social media as a research tool and for searching for people on Facebook if I look for potential interviewees. And I also use Twitter, but I am not very content about Twitter. I am very much sporadic in how I use it".[23] Another male foreign correspondent remarked on the tension between using social media and bolstering old journalistic practices, including verification:

> I use cell phones pictures particularly at the beginning of those stories. That is happening at the time that we do not have our own camera there or it is too dangerous to get our own camera's there. There are times when that type of material is absolutely essential. There are times when it is almost better than good quality material. If feels real. You have to be careful. You will hear, you cannot verify it. You have to be more careful on how to use it, but it is important.[24]

Journalists such as Silvia Costeloe also use direct sources with the help of the UGC Hub staff, who help gather sources in a centralised fashion:

> So often when there's a breaking story, often it is just pictures that are needed. So if we find the pictures on the web, we get permission. I mean depending on what kind of story it is, whether we feel that it's covered by fair use or not. Obviously if it's stills it isn't. So we try to get—and talk to people, and first of all get their permission to run the pictures. So we might have, in many instances, the first pictures these days that come out are user-generated pictures.
>
> (Silvia Costeloe quoted in Stray, 2010)

Similarly, a male foreign correspondent reported that he uses social media as a direct source of information within the centralised UGC Hub. As an Assistant Editor at the UGC Hub stated, this practice enables journalists to gather news faster:

> Say the Haiti earthquake when that happened. One of the first thing that our producers did it. And it happened over night—and we only have one producer at night. But she started looking across blogs, blogs about Haiti, Twitter accounts on Haiti—and very quickly found example of people who were in Haiti and who were experiencing the earthquake and were tweeting about it. So she got in touch with them, got their contact details, checked them out, made sure they were authentic, and then put them on air. And that happened an hour from the earthquake happening. And in the old days that would have been impossible to do that—because we have no reporter in Haiti. It would have taken

long time to send a reporter there. And trying to find these case studies of contact would have taken several hours. For example, if that had happened before we would have to get through eyewitness to the story, which would never be possible.[25]

Similarly, in an interview, a male foreign correspondent reported that he did not use social media. He stated, "I don't actually. I probably should. During the Haiti earthquake I remember following a few twitter feeds. They just helped giving a picture of what was going on".[26] Costeloe says that in the past, journalists relied to a greater extent on old media such as *The New York Times*. Journalists took stories from that newspaper:

> I would look at *The New York Times* and I would take stories from there. I had to broaden the range of publication to generate stories ideas. You listened to radio, watched three television stations, read Newsweek (almost went out of business) and *The New York Times* (now struggling)— all of which are under pressure.
>
> (Silvia Costeloe quoted in Stray, 2010)

Kevin Bakhurst, former Controller of BBC News Channel and Deputy Head of the BBC Newsroom, corroborated the statements made above by foreign correspondents. In a formal speech made on behalf of the news organisation, Bakhurst wrote that social media are a democratising force that "helps us gather more, and sometimes better, material; we can find a wider ranges of voices, ideas and eyewitnesses quickly" (Bakhurst, 2011). A male foreign correspondent added, "sometimes you can get the information faster on Twitter than any other newswires, although you have to be sceptical about it. We all tweet and post messages on Facebook. A lot of it is still at a personal level".[27] The centralised UGC Hub finds most of the social media material. Journalists can also seek social media sources individually.

Social Media as a Source of Stories

Social media also became a source of stories for BBC journalists. For example, a female foreign correspondent stated,

> The only other thing I would say is that we cover lots of social media stories like Facebook in terms of the business and we interview some of the people who are involved but . . . it is quite a specialised field. If you tweet about revolutions, you are not going to tweet about the results of Coca Cola in quite the same way.[28]

A male foreign correspondent revealed how social media turned out to be a story in itself:

> We did just an awareness piece that the reason of that site that managed to be so successful is that they get people to interact. It is not an

aggregated site, but it is a news, views and opinion website and that was quite interesting that somebody like AOL old fashion possibly dying organisation got involved in something very much at the forefront. A lot of people are critical of the Huffington Post because it actually links to a lot of other things. There is journalism on the website and picking stuff from others which obviously going to make your site more attracting if you take the best of the best.[29]

Likewise, during the 2009 Iranian election, BBC Technology reporter Maggie Shiels (2009) wrote an online piece about how Twitter users responded to the censorship role of the Iranian government in the election. Shiels pointed out that in these cases, social media became the story. Similarly, in an interview, a female foreign correspondent stated, "For work, if I use social media for researching stories and get in touch with people. It may start with a search on Google, then Facebook or LinkedIn or I may be reading articles through Twitter that linked me to an article".[30] Illustrating a similar point, a male foreign correspondent stated that during the Arab Spring he covered a story that emerged from a Facebook page about missing people in Egypt. One day during the Egyptian revolution, the journalist and several colleagues stumbled upon a Facebook page dedicated to a missing Egyptian protestor. Journalists thus developed a series of news pieces on the topic of missing people in Egypt.[31]

In sum, since the emergence of social media, journalists have integrated social media sourcing into their preexisting sourcing routine and included a greater range of social media sources in international crisis reporting. Rather than solely consisting of a direct source or a way of accessing a network of sources, social media are an indirect source of news stories. There is strong evidence that journalists perceive and manage sources within traditional journalistic norms and practices. Within this media logic journalists are learning to manage the tension between old and new media.

The Hierarchy of Sources

Johan Galtung and Mari Holmboe Ruge (1965) demonstrated that journalists in foreign news in Norway employed 12 factors to determine the newsworthiness of a story: frequency, threshold, unambiguity, meaningfulness, consonance, unexpectedness, continuity, compositional balance, elite nations and regions, personification, and negativity. Galtung and Ruge suggested the "additivity hypothesis": the more news value an event has, the more likely it will become news. In his newsroom ethnography of American print and broadcast mainstream news media, American sociologist Herbert Gans (1979) suggested that the status and prestige of the source remain important factors in newsworthiness. The traditional hierarchy of sources continues to be applied in the work of journalists at the BBC in social media contexts.

The BBC journalists I interviewed emphasised four main criteria for assessing the relevance of sources on social media. First, journalists judge sources on their geographical proximity. Second, journalists consider the authoritativeness, past suitability, productivity, and reliability of a source. Third, journalists look at sources' previous attachment to prestigious or recognised institutions. Fourth, journalists assess the trustworthiness and accuracy of a source. These four criteria suggest that journalists process information from social media sources in much the same way they process information from other sources in the daily cycle. Each of these criteria will be described in more detail below.

First, international correspondents use news sources relevant to their geographical proximity. For instance, Los Angeles-based foreign correspondents often focus their attention on the *Los Angeles Times*, whereas New York-based correspondents read *The Wall Street Journal* or *The New York Times* to a greater extent.

Second, journalists draw a line between institutional and personal social media sources. Institutional social media sources tend to receive more interest and credibility from journalists. For example, a World Affairs unit reporter and Producer said,

> It is not so much criteria set. But it is based on merit. For example, if it is somebody who got a prestigious rank or something like that. We don't get the president of the U.S. very easily, but if you got somebody with some kind of title—like we are trying to get an interview with the Euro director for the International Monetary Fund (IMF). If we get that, then it will probably be interesting for the domestic outlets as well.

Several journalists in my interviews reported that they evaluate the relevance of a source on its authoritativeness, past suitability, productivity, reliability, and trustworthiness. Most foreign correspondents stated that they use institutional blogs such as those at Politico.com, an American website owned by Allbritton Communications Company and affiliated with ABC since 1997,[32] and at *The New York Times*. Business news journalists consulted *The Wall Street Journal*, a newspaper that stores most of its articles behind a paywall, a mechanism that prevents Internet users from accessing an online news story without a paid subscription. Besides social media, journalists mentioned they employed other news media sources to put a story together: These include newspapers, magazines, and wire services (e.g., Reuters, Agence France Press, and Associated Press). Journalists read newspapers and magazines online on their computers, on their mobile devices, and on paper. International business correspondents I interviewed who were based in the United States said they relied heavily on the online and paper versions of *The Wall Street Journal*, *The Economist*, and the *Financial Times*.

Journalists also mentioned using personal blogs and aggregation sites as sources of information. Blogs include those of Andrew Sullivan and *The Huffington Post*—the latter bought in 2011 by AOL. Competition influences the degree and intensity of use of sources. For example, as one editor in the newsroom said, "[i]f all the other mainstream media outlets talk about it, it might be an important story". Reporters are thus more likely to use sources that are suitable to their audiences, mindful of the herd mentality. Earlier sociological analyses have considered the suitability of sources (Galtung and Ruge, 1965; Gans, 1979; Molotch and Lester, 1974). Dominic L. Lasorsa, Seth C. Lewis, and Avery E. Holton also discovered that journalists on Twitter linked to more prestigious outlets. They wrote, "Perhaps the more 'elite' media are less inclined to share opinions, engage readers, and so forth, because they believe they have so much vested in business as usual" (Lasorsa, Lewis, and Holton, 2012, 31). This tendency may also be explained by the fact that less relevant sources must try harder to make an impact on social media.

Third, journalists relied on social media sources attached to prestigious news organisations. In interviews, journalists reported that they value social media sources that influence major news organisations, such as *The New York Times*. Trustworthiness and accuracy of information remain important news selection criteria. A female foreign correspondent stated,

> If you know the individual and if you trust the people that you are following on Twitter, it is your own judgement. I know people from other media organisations in the United States that tweet prolifically. I do not necessarily trust if it is people that I do not know. You can use Twitter as a guide. If a lot of people say the same thing, it cannot be bad. There is something happening. But you still want to check it out and confirm by yourself.[33]

Writing about the UGC Hub, Kevin Bakhurst argues that accuracy is a crucial value when journalists have to assess social media sources:

> The team we have allows us to fully engage in using this material, and reinforce the BBC values that our audience expects, in particular accuracy. So we managed to avoid, for example, use of the photo-shopped bin Laden body photo after his killing.
>
> (Bakhurst, 2011)

Fourth, accuracy and verification of sources are key tenets favoured by BBC journalism, and this is reflected in news production practices and editorial decisions. For example, social media brought new verification practices. Alex Murray, UGC Hub Producer, stated, "[a]t the UGC Hub in the BBC Newsroom in London, our process has become much more forensic in nature" (Murray, 2011). He adds,

> Regardless of provenance—from the most established source to the individual who has only ever uploaded one clip—everything we see goes through the verification process before we give our opinion on it. If it

says it comes from the social media sphere, we question it until we're happy that the claims being made stack up.

(Murray, 2011)

Accuracy remains a central principle in BBC journalism:

> Journalists still have to do the good old fashioned newsgathering job of checking out sources, getting the story themselves and then using the UGC material as added value, as extra stuff that can help them to do their job but not do the job for them.
>
> (Hugh Berlyn, Senior Online Editor, quoted in Wardle and Williams, 2010)

Social media platforms have their advantages for reporters. For example, Facebook helped journalists gain faster and easier access to networks of sources, texts, videos, audio, and pictures of news characters. Journalists are aware of the importance of social media as a source, and the different uses of individual social media platforms. Whereas there are important differences between traditional sourcing and social media sourcing, social media sources fit within the existing newsgathering structure, which has established news values and selection criteria. Similarly, in the case of the 2009 Iran election, Danish news coverage and mediation of citizen material also turned to sourcing as a strategy for mimicking the traditional modes of journalistic sourcing. Andersen contends that

> markers of the sourcing strategy are double: a combination of an absence of explicit doubt in the source and an explicit reference to some kind of contextual information intended to allow the reader some (albeit often carefully selected and not unbiased) information against which to assess the credibility, bias, authority etc. of the referred source.
>
> (Andersen, 2012)

BBC journalists stated that traditional news values, norms, and practices thus continue to serve as the lenses through which journalists evaluate social media sources daily, although they have to take into account social media in their reporting. At the same time, these news values are articulated in the new communication infrastructure involving social media, both as content and activity.

NEWS DISTRIBUTION

Besides their role at the BBC as journalistic tools for newsgathering, crowdsourcing, and monitoring the news, social media have started to rival online searches as a way for audiences to find news content (Newman, 2011). The

Corporation turned to social media as an instrument to distribute and market its news stories.[34] BBC journalists can distribute, share, and market news on social media to audiences in a variety of ways. First, journalists disseminate the news via institutional accounts such as Twitter (e.g., @bbcbreaking, @bbcworld, @bbcnews), Facebook (e.g., BBC World News, BBC Radio 1, BBC Persian, BBC News, BBC Urdu), and Google+ (e.g., BBC America, BBC News, BBC Click, BBC World Have Your Say, Rory Cellan-Jones). Methods of sharing vary across social media networks. For example, people share funny and unusual stories on Facebook. On Twitter, users contribute to more serious and running news stories (Newman, 2011, 24). Second, individual BBC journalists, such as @pdanahar, @Trushar, and @WilliamsJon, share the news. Likewise, a Welsh Online News Editor stated,

> The other thing I think that we will increasingly focus on is using social media as a way of delivering BBC news content to potential new audiences that you would not have had access before. We are getting a whole generation of people now who are very digitally savvy—and it is not unusual for them to be. They have a smart mobile phone, engage people through social media sites. As that type of technology develop it becomes more natural for people. We need to make sure that we are meeting and anticipating audiences' expectations of how you are going to conceive BBC news content. Before people would sit down and listen to the Six O'clock News or Ten O'clock News in the evening—watch the news bulletin. These audiences remain strong. But there exists other sort of experiences news consumption, which is becoming more the behaviour now. People consuming news once they are on the news on different platforms, with different technologies. That's one of our key challenge in delivering that content in changing way, but still retaining our BBC values and brand which is trusted and not become diluted in term of our work just because the technology is developing so quickly.[35]

Third, BBC audiences disseminate the news on social media platforms. The growth of social media activities has given a platform for reporters to share their work and the work of others online. Twitter and Facebook drive traffic to the BBC website. From 2009 to 2011, "The number of click-throughs to the BBC from Facebook increased by over 400 per cent" (Newman, 2011, 15). For instance, 20 years after the Serbo-Croat conflict, BBC World Affairs unit Producer Stuart Hughes used social media to promote a story on Croatia. This story is relevant because it demonstrates how journalists can use social media as a distribution tool for news content.

In 2011, Stuart Hughes travelled to Croatia with BBC special correspondent Allan Little. Little had first visited the Balkans in 1991 to cover the escalating violence between Croats and Serbs. He went there for what was supposed to be a two-week trip and stayed in the region for four years. In 2011, Little returned to Croatia with Hughes to cover what had happened to the country between the end of the war in 1991 and its entry into the European Union. While there, Hughes thought that the material the two journalists were shooting for Radio Four, the Ten O'clock News, and Online News would become a compelling news piece (Hugues, 2011).

Hughes asked, "how can we build a little bit of momentum on the story?". Then, "how can we alert people that we are working on a good news piece?". Hughes subsequently "assembled a trail and pushed it through YouTube" (Hughes, 2011). He edited the piece on his way from Vukovar to Zagreb, in the back of the car. Hughes then sent a Tweet to approximately 20 influential tweeters. In doing so, he spread the word and generated pre-publicity for the piece. These influential tweeters included former BBC social media trainer, external consultant, and academic Claire Wardle,[36] who he thought would disseminate the story to the appropriate audiences.

The BBC twitter feed (@BBCNews) also promoted the piece by directing followers to the YouTube link rather than by re-tweeting Hughes's message. In addition to independent and BBC-approved social media accounts, the Corporation used several institutional Twitter accounts where these messages could be posted. These accounts included @BBCBreaking (6,649,304 followers), @BBCWorld (4,107,429 followers), and @BBCNews (UK) (1,800,447 followers).[37] These three accounts are linked to the BBC Live Event online pages, related stories webpages, and BBC correspondents' official webpages. Journalists used each of these accounts to disseminate Hughes's tweet promising that a news piece was coming out in a week on the Ten O'clock News.

A week later, on the day of the news broadcast about Croatia, Hughes continued to distribute the news using social media. He chose a picture from Croatia in 1992 and "twitpiced" it. Since 2008, Twitpic has operated as a social media website that enables users to share photos and videos as they happen. These photos and videos are distributed to Twitter and other social media platforms. On Twitter, Hughes wrote that the full story would be revealed that night on the Ten O'clock News. By discussing the story before its broadcast, Hughes hoped to draw viewers who would not otherwise watch the programme. Additionally, Hughes said he hoped that viewers would watch the show because of the discussion on Twitter about the Croatia story (Hughes, 2011).

Journalists such as Hughes use social media to distribute and promote BBC journalism, hoping to generate new audiences from social media for the BBC traditional news outlets. Hughes employed social media to distribute and market his news piece. He did this by adding multimedia value (with Twitpic), using BBC official and nonofficial Twitter accounts to disseminate the news, and working with influential tweeters he knew to drive audiences to BBC news outlets.

Importantly, journalistic uses of social media differ according to the age of the reporter. Younger journalists, such as Hughes, are more likely to use social media as an extension of their personal and professional communication. By contrast, at first, many older journalists did not think social media were necessary and were reluctant to embrace them as journalistic tools. Hughes was one of the first BBC bloggers and said that he had an easy time learning to use new social media tools. Since 2010, the guidance on social media has distinguished between institutional and non-institutional BBC social media accounts. Hughes was an early adopter because he knew the software and the news, and quickly developed an understanding of what social media could do for BBC news distribution.

It is also important to highlight that different guidelines exist for personal and professional accounts. Personal accounts are not official and are not fully part of the BBC. Even though those accounts do not have official status, journalists who wish to have them must gain permission from their line manager "to ensure that impartiality and confidentiality is maintained" (BBC, 2011). These guidelines refer mainly to not putting the BBC into disrepute, being sensitive with comments, and not conflating journalists' personal views with those of the news organisation. For instance, on Twitter, many journalists wrote in their personal description that what they say on that account "does not reflect the opinion of the BBC". Likewise, many journalists wrote, "re-tweets are not endorsements". Since 2011, the BBC has labelled official journalists' accounts on Twitter. The Corporation regulates these accounts with clear expectations and rules. The BBC expects that journalists who use these accounts will act "within the context of their role at the BBC" and not as a distinct personal platform. The journalists who hold official accounts tend to be more active professionally on social media platforms. By contrast, many who do not have official accounts mentioned that they were not very active on social media.

Another instance of distribution via social media occurred during my fieldwork in January 2011. Online news distribution occurred particularly on Twitter. On 15 August 2010 in the province of Kunduz, located in northern Afghanistan, a man and a woman were accused of having an adulterous affair. They were stoned to death in a crowded bazaar (BBC, 2010). Months later, on 19 January 2011, BBC journalists found an online post containing a video of the stoning. A Newsgathering editor came to the Ten O'clock News desk to talk about a story regarding the Taliban killing of an adulterous Afghan couple. Throughout the day, in the multimedia newsroom, editors held multiple closed-door meetings to discuss producing a news piece on the killings. A senior manager and two editors congregated in an office to decide if the BBC would broadcast the video on the news that day. The team finally decided not to broadcast on either the Six O'clock News or the Ten O'clock News.

According to a Six O'clock News and Ten O'clock News Editor, showing the video was not justifiable editorially.[38] Several factors led to that decision. There are multiple levels of regulation at the BBC, such as the BBC Trust and Ofcom, the Independent regulator and competition authority for the United Kingdom communications industry.[39] Ofcom regulates the watershed, which is also emulated in the BBC Editorial Guidelines. The television watershed, from 9 p.m. to 5:30 a.m., refers to a time block for material not suitable for children. The regulator Ofcom determines the watershed rule, which also appears in the BBC Editorial Guidelines.[40] In the Afghan couple stoning case, an editor recalled five editorial disagreements involving the watershed time block: the origins of the video, the nature of the story, what section should they show of the material, the threshold (what is appropriate or not), and the power of the story. That story had already been reported back in August 2010. But there was no video available at the time. Because the video was available online, it was not breaking news. "Editorially, it was not well-founded to broadcast it".[41] The team finally decided that because the video was already online on another website that day, there was no justification to put it on television.

Although rules influence journalists' uses of social media material, journalists at the Six O'clock News and Ten O'clock News were divided on whether the BBC should air the video of the Afghan couple. On the one hand, some journalists promoted the editorial stance mentioned above. On the other hand, in the meeting, a news presenter questioned this decision, arguing that because news can come online first, journalists need to adapt their editorial process and understanding of ethics to this new reality. In the end, the BBC Online team covered the story, but the BBC did not post the video on its website.

While this debate was going on in the newsroom, a journalist disseminated the news on Twitter. Jon Williams, World News Editor, started the distribution process by tweeting: "Today we revisit the tragedy of young couple stoned to death in Afghanistan for 'adultery.' Shocking images of Taliban justice as crowd watch". Much like a tweet sent by Stuart Hughes when he was in Croatia, this tweet marketed a future news piece. After the meeting, Williams wrote on Twitter, personalising his tweet: "Clearly many issues for us before we broadcast stoning of Afghan couple. Full video horrific, but excerpts show operation of Taliban justice". Williams's tweet reflected what was happening in the newsroom and the editorial decision-making process.

Williams also added multimedia value by distributing the link to the BBC Online article: "After 1st public stoning in Afghanistan since 2001 we revisit story of couple executed for adultery by Taliban http://bbc.in/cLL6he". Adding multimedia value means adding multimedia applications (audio, videos, or images) on social networking websites. Audio applications include: Audioboo (application for your mobile website to record and upload audio, text, and images to your tweets), Chir.ps (for recording), Twaud.io (for uploading audio to TI, sending an e-mail from an iPhone), Tinysong Groveeshark (for linking to songs), and Tweetmic (for recording and uploading audio, and recording "Tweetcasts"). Image applications include Twitpic (an application for Twitter that has its own iPhone application), Twitprix (to share pictures on the web, e-mail, and phone), Twicsy (image search engine for Twitter enabling users to upload images), Plixi (formerly TweetPhto), and Yfrog. Video applications include Bubbletweet (to create a video appearance; it appears as a bubble above Twitter users' profile pictures), Pickhur, Tvider, Screenr, and Twitcam (part of Livestream; these allow users to connect a webcam and stream live videos to Twitter). Note that since 2012, the BBC has maintained an official partnership with Audioboo for publishing web clips and content. In this case of the reportage of the stoning, Williams added value to his tweet by including a link to the article on the BBC website and by distributing a link to the piece via Twitter.

In this case, BBC social media representatives and editors were capable of influencing journalistic uses of social media. According to the BBC social media guidances (2011), each division has a social media representative that Interactive editors and senior editors keep informed of relevant activities. Social media representatives and editors manage the risks and share social media experiences with BBC divisions. Here we observe the important role of editorial expectations. Journalists deal with those expectations on a daily basis. For instance, in the example of the stoning video, one editorial expectation addresses three ideas: that is, taste, standards, and quality. These three ideas refer to the values and aesthetic of behaviour in journalistic practice. For instance, the social media guidances suggest that journalists may need to apply "light touch" with social media material that they use in packaged news pieces:

> So there are some circumstances where the BBC will need to plan and implement an additional 'light touch' intervention, for example to remove comments which are likely to cause extreme offence. We will need to work out how this should be done, who will do it and when. Where necessary, Editorial Policy can advise on a suitable threshold for 'light touch' intervention. Recent research suggests that this approach matches audience expectations. One problem is that while social networking sites may publish clear rules of acceptable behaviour for their users, they are often very reluctant to share much information about how they intervene or to what level.
>
> (BBC, 2010)

If journalists are not familiar with certain social networking website practices—for example, how they should deal with harmful or illegal content—the guidelines recommend that journalists seek advice with the Central Community team in Future Media & Technology. Similarly, in 2005, Ofcom published the Code of Standards in broadcasting, stating that content must not be harmful or offensive. Mirroring Ofcom regulations, the BBC states that social media have their own rules and guidelines, which might not be the same as those of the Corporation. Journalists must apply light touch to social media content before publishing it. Together, the social media guidelines, Ofcom, and BBC journalists have built a flexible framework for journalistic uses of social media within the context of BBC public service reporting.

These two cases of journalistic experiences with social media highlight how news dissemination on social media can lead to greater engagement between the BBC and audiences, and a different mode of storytelling. These cases also demonstrate that disseminating news by social media involves a set of questions about journalists' perception and management of the structure and guidelines of the organisation. These cases show that social media enable a new form of broadcasting news (input and output), involving a new set of practices and norms building on "old" ones.[42] Importantly, as I describe the actors involved in the process, we notice that tech-savvy journalists have become crucial in shaping the meaning of social media at the public broadcaster. These journalists select content and contribute to the production of crisis reporting. This dynamic will be the main focus of the next chapter.

FROM "SHOULD WE?" TO "HOW SHOULD WE?"

The role of social media in BBC journalism is part of a process of renegotiation involving journalists, managers, broadcasting policies, audiences, new information technologies, formats, as well as journalistic structures, practices, and norms in crisis reporting and in everyday reporting. In 2012, the BBC updated its social media guidelines, for example. BBC editors instructed their journalists not to break news stories on Twitter before first talking to their newsroom colleagues. These guidelines insisted that journalists seek a second pair of eyes before updating messages on Twitter or Facebook (Sonderman, 2011). Also, Sky News banned its journalists from reposting on Twitter information that originated outside the news organisation (Plunkett, 2012). For both BBC News and Sky News, such policies meant that the organisation's newsgathering machine would determine which stories are covered.

In crisis reporting events, journalists have reaffirmed their norms and practices in the new media logic consisting of increasing audience participation and social media. "There is something to be said about the changing working conditions of journalists in different industries that are merging and to some extent collaborating in an attempt to reach new and especially younger audiences, while at the same time maintaining their privileged position in society", wrote Mark Deuze (2008, 5). The evolution of social media in BBC journalism is part of a larger institutional and cultural shift in which the news organisation is becoming a leader in new technologies in the United Kingdom, sustaining its impartiality and collaborating increasingly with its audiences.

NOTES

1. Fieldwork notes, January 2011.
2. POLIS is the research hub located in the department of media and communications at the London School of Economics.
3. The fact that journalism is conducted on social media posed challenges during my fieldwork. Ethnography of the newsroom is no longer confined to newsrooms or innovation processes. Researchers need to study the newsroom beyond its physical entity, and need to analyse a broader set of interactions across an often geographically dispersed media system.
4. Fieldwork notes, January 2011.
5. Carvin, e-mail exchange 2012.
6. Carvin, e-mail exchange 2012.
7. UGC Hub Manager, BBC, interview 2011.
8. UGC Hub Manager, BBC, interview 2011.
9. Andy Carvin, NPR, e-mail exchange 2012 and UGC Hub journalist, BBC, interview 2011.
10. Carvin, e-mail exchange 2012.
11. Fieldwork in the Middle East would have provided further evidence of the role of social media in networked journalism.
12. BBC journalist/trainer/editor currently heading up Digital + Social Media training for the College of Journalism, interview 2012.
13. BBC journalist/trainer/editor currently heading up Digital + Social Media training for the College of Journalism, interview 2012.
14. In August 2012 Steve Myers became the Deputy Managing Editor and Senior Staff writer for The Lens, a nonprofit investigative news site in New Orleans, United States.
15. Additional case studies can prompt further reflections on the power dynamics at play during these events, not simply at the BBC but also in the global media ecosystem.
16. Six and Ten O'clock News Editor, interview 2011.
17. International business correspondent, interview 2011.
18. Male foreign correspondent, interview 2011.
19. World Affairs unit Producer, interview 2011.
20. Six and Ten O'Clock News Editor, interview 2011.
21. Female foreign correspondent, interview 2011.
22. Female foreign correspondent, interview 2011.
23. Male foreign correspondent, interview 2011.
24. Male foreign correspondent, interview 2011.
25. Assistant Editor UGC Hub, interview 2011.
26. Male foreign correspondent, interview 2011.
27. Male foreign correspondent, interview 2011.
28. Female foreign correspondent, interview 2011.
29. Male foreign correspondent, interview 2011.
30. Female foreign correspondent, interview 2011.
31. Male foreign correspondent, interview 2011.
32. Politico.com possesses a print outlet, but most of its readership is derived from more than six million online visitors per month.
33. Female foreign correspondent, interview 2011.
34. Social media and editorial journalist, interview 2011.
35. Online News Editor Wales, interview 2011.
36. As of 2014, Claire Wardle works for Storyful.

37. These numbers were first collected on Thursday, 29 November 2012 and updated on 2 August 2013.
38. Six and Ten O'clock News Editor, interview 2011.
39. Financed by fees from the industry and accountable to the Parliament, Ofcom is the Office of Communications established on 29 December 2003 under the Communications Act 2003 taking upon the work of five regulators: the Broadcasting Standards Commission, the Independent Television Commission, the Office of Telecommunications (Oftel), the Radio Authority, and the Radiocommunications Agency.
40. The watershed does not apply to radio.
41. Six and Ten O'clock News Editor, interview 2011.
42. Note that British law also contributes to the uses of social media in news production. This has been the case notably since the publication of the Neil Report in 2004. The Report stipulated that editorial lawyers would need to "be present in the newsroom with journalists" (Neil, 2004, 22). For instance, the social media guidelines stipulate that journalists should be mindful of legal implications when using social media, because of copyright laws (BBC, 2010). During my fieldwork in the production control room, just before the Ten O'clock News went on the air, a producer prevented a Facebook picture from being used because the third party owning the picture did not grant the rights. Journalists are aware that broadcasting a picture can have defamation and privacy implications. For example, a journalist said, "account holders put pictures of themselves drinking with their friends, with bottles in their mouth to portray themselves as party animals. When we are faced with this kind of picture, we ask: what would the family think, do they want to be commemorated that way . . . If we have the choice of images, we would tend to go for ones that would portray the person on a more favourable way" (Online News Editor Wales, interview 2011). There are nevertheless times when legal implications and the BBC public service ethos can be combined. Blogger Andy Mabett complained that the BBC had used the Houla massacre photographs without naming the people who took those photographs, thus breaching copyright laws. A few days later, on the BBC editors' blog, Chris Hamilton confirmed that the BBC made efforts to contact people who had taken photos, and had asked permission to use the pictures. However, journalists can decide to publish a photo before clearing it, especially if the photo is of "strong public interest" and the photo needs to be made available to a wide audience. In this quote, the public interest argument comes from the Reynolds defence or privilege (Reynolds v Times Newspapers Ltd.), which protects publication of defamatory material if the subject matter is of public interest and the journalist acted responsibly. Chris Hamilton wrote, "So, when we can't credit the copyright holder, our practice has been to label the photo to indicate where it was obtained, such as 'From Twitter', as part of our normal procedure for sourcing content used in our output (Hamilton, 2011b). Journalists need to negotiate issues related to users and publishers' intentions and consent, impact of reuse of pictures, and legal issues when dealing with social media on a daily basis. Note on the Reynolds defence: Albert Reynolds was the Prime Minister of Ireland when the *Times* published an article in Ireland and then in the United Kingdom stating that Reynolds had misled the Irish Parliament. In the UK, the article did not add Reynolds's version of the events. Incidentally, Reynolds brought Times Newspapers Ltd. to court. The case therefore concerned qualified privilege for the publication of defamatory statements that are of public interest. Following this case, journalists have had the duty to publish a statement even though it might be false. The following case, *Jameel v Wall Street Journal Europe*, cemented the defence in libel cases. The Defamation Bill

2012–13 section 4(5) stated (December 2012) that the "common law defence known as the Reynolds defence is abolished" (Defamation HL Bill (2012–13) [75]). In February 2013, public interest defence (now clause 6 rather than 4) read: "(1) It is a defence to an action for defamation for the defendant to show that (a) the statement complained of was, or formed part of, a statement on a matter of public interest; and (b) the defendant reasonably believed that publishing the statement complained of was in the public interest. (2) Subject to subsections (3) and (4) in determining whether the defendant has shown the matters mentioned in subsection (1) the court must have regard to all the circumstances of the case" (Defamation HL Bill (2012–13) [139]). The case kept the public interest defence but even though rejecting Reynolds kept the principle alive. The third reading of the law was scheduled for 25 February 2013 before going in front of the House of Commons.

4 New Structures, New Actors in the Newsrooms

> All big news organisations are plunging into the world of social media, looking at its extraordinary newsgathering potential; its potential as a new tool to engage the audience; and as a way of distributing our news.
>
> (Kevin Bakhurst, former Deputy Head of the BBC newsroom, 2011)

THE NEW GENERATION OF TECHIES

The values of egalitarianism and subjectivity compete with traditional journalistic values of control, filtering, and impartiality. For example, journalists have incorporated citizen eyewitness accounts within the norm of impartiality. This incorporation still represents a great challenge for a BBC rooted in the vision of first General Manager John Reith of educating, informing, and entertaining. Since the London bombing attacks, the volume of user-generated content has grown dramatically in a short period of time. This change in the dynamic of the organisation has, in turn, raised expectations from BBC audiences, dissolving the boundaries between journalists and their audiences (Jones and Salter, 2012, 85).

This chapter looks beyond the journalistic uses of social media at the BBC. In this chapter, I explore how tech-savvy journalists are becoming pioneers in crisis reporting, which is increasingly connected to its audiences. I analyse the role played by these techies in articulating journalism in social media contexts. For the BBC, this process has involved changed working relations among colleagues in the newsroom and with audiences, while preserving its authority as a public broadcaster. By gaining knowledge of social media, tech-savvy journalists have created structures that enable a new, increasingly participatory form of crisis reporting.

THE NEWS CYCLE AND SOCIAL MEDIA

Structure: The Centralisation of Social Media Deployment

At the BBC, the UGC Hub centrally manages social media. This Hub is located within the Newsgathering unit[1] in the multimedia newsroom. At first glance, social media are wedded to the Hub. But in practice, social media alliances in BBC journalism are much more intricate than an initial glance conveys. The UGC Hub was created in 2005, shortly after the 7 July London bombing attacks, in response to increasing public usage of social media for news. Since 2007–2008, the UGC Hub has been located at the centre of the multimedia newsroom on the first floor of the Television Centre. The Hub emerged from the online news operation BBC Interactive, which was initially located on the 7th floor of the Television Centre. In 2009, the UGC Hub became responsible for social media and operated within the Newsgathering unit section called the Newswire Hub, which breaks news within the newsroom and among BBC journalists worldwide. The Newswire Hub stands in the centre of the multimedia newsroom, between the United Kingdom team, World News, and BBC News 24, and includes Newswire and Mediaport operations. Mediaport brings together all recording operations and pictures from across the organisation into a coordinated operation. The Newswire unit consists of a monitoring service. Journalists in the Newswire unit record incoming feeds as well as alerts, and write headlines.

Within the BBC general structure,[2] the UGC Hub has acted as consolidator, processing technologies such as digital videos and images, mobile text messages, blogging content, message boards, e-mails, audio material generated by the audience, and other social media-related activities. These activities are centralised in the Hub because the news organisation needs to "have people who find those pictures, and find those eyewitness accounts, and then farm them out to output. So give them to TV, give them to radio, give them to online, and sort of make sure that, you know, the story being told across all our several platforms", said Silvia Costeloe, broadcast journalist, UGC Hub (quoted in Stray, 2010).

The centralisation of social media in the UGC Hub activities has encouraged the efficient use of resources in BBC journalism. For example, the Hub has reduced the cost of materials to cover the same news event (Chouliaraki, 2010b; Bruns, 2008; Turner, 2010).[3] At the same time, social media allow journalists to cover events where no journalists are present. Costeloe highlights how this dynamic plays out in the newsroom:

> To have it centralised is really useful, especially when it comes to breaking stories, because, you know, our reporters . . . might not be living somewhere, so they'll have to travel somewhere, and in the meantime we're doing lots of newsgathering, we're giving them contacts of people on the ground. . . . Recently there was a story, a big explosion in

Connecticut, and within an hour of the explosion there was a Facebook group devoted to the explosion, and the families of the explosion,
because no one really knew what was going on. So that proved to be a
really good source of newsgathering.

(Costeloe quoted in Stray, 2010)

According to Costeloe, one of the main advantages of the UGC Hub is
that there is a "possibility to go more in-depth in some stories" (quoted
in Stray, 2010). However, as a Senior Manager at BBC World Service and
Global News stated,[4] some journalists perceive the UGC Hub as a challenge,
because the centralised focus on big, breaking stories limits the number of
stories the BBC will cover.[5] The structure of the newsroom and the positioning of social media activities within the UGC Hub signal the centrality of
citizen material in news production. This structure has far-reaching implications for the BBC's uses of social media in reporting.

The configuration of the multimedia newsroom and the centralisation
of the User-Generated Content Hub have affected news production by staff
who work in the newsroom. This staff gained influence in the newsroom
in a short amount of time by its physical positioning in the newsroom. For
instance, in 2011, the Six O'clock News and Ten O'clock News desk enjoyed
a strategic location next to the domestic deployment facilities and the newswire service, the BBC's internal newswire agency. This newsroom configuration gave journalists from Six O'clock News and Ten O'clock News easy
physical access to the UGC Hub. Because of the multilayered structure of
the news organisation, BBC journalists also managed social media using
channels of communication outside the UGC Hub. English Regions, BBC
Sports, and World Service (including BBC Arabic) have their own social
media strategy programmes.[6] By creating a need for oversight, social media
led to the formation of new structures to manage the new media. Since
the Six O'clock News and Ten O'clock News team has moved to the New
Broadcasting House in early 2012, the proximity of the UGC Hub to the
team is comparable.

BBC journalists can use social media as part of the BBC's official social
media presence and/or separately from the BBC. For example, in 2011, BBC
Wales hired its first Social Media Editor. Some journalists also have an offi-
cial BBC Twitter account, whereas others use their personal Facebook or
Twitter account to find sources for news stories. Journalists also manage
social media through other outputs, which include TV, radio, and online.
For example, journalists can share content using the central Journalism
Portal (J-Portal). Launched in November 2010 as a two-year project, the
J-Portal is organised around editorial communities, which include the UK
and niche areas or communities of interests for the news organisation. It
is an interactive space to share ideas, thoughts, and questions. Each story
community possesses its own page where it can discuss the latest breaking
news for its coverage and Twitter comments (Barrett, 2011). For example,

a journalist interested in reporting on a topic related to Africa could use the portal to access a chat room and community in which users share and search for information with people who are logged in at the same time.[7] Although social media uses are centralised within the UGC Hub page of the portal, social media are also integrated in the outputs, programmes, and daily deliveries portal pages.

Whereas the news organisation is managed around the BBC General Manager, as of 2014 social media are integrated within the hierarchical structure, particularly in newsgathering through the UGC Hub. As a result, journalists are dependent on the expertise of the UGC Hub to provide them with social media content, although journalists can use social media without the direct support of the Hub.[8] The BBC has adjusted its use of social media within its existing model. Within this structure, social media usage is centralised primarily within the UGC Hub, as a newsgathering tool.

The existence of centralised social media management within the Hub since 2005, along with various crisis news events, demonstrates how social media created a demand. At the same time, the BBC responded by creating a centralised structure within the newsroom to deal with social media. And tech-savvy journalists quickly gained power within an "old" structure. Yet the structure of the newsroom is only one facet of news production. The planning and daily cycle, within the structure of the newsroom, and the role that social media have taken on in the years since 7/7 are other important facets of news production.

Daily Cycle and Planning: A Day During the Tunisian Uprising

The cycle follows into a pattern of journalistic work. Within that cycle, social media plays an important role. This pattern of work is a series of phases, planning, and daily deliveries.[9] The daily news intake involves a sequence of official meetings. The first meeting each day is the morning editorial meeting; at 8 a.m., chaired by a senior figure in Newsgathering, the morning editorial meeting begins. This is followed by the news board meeting at 8:40 a.m., chaired by the BBC News Director or the Deputy Director BBC News and Head of Multimedia Programs.

Every morning at 9 a.m., the editors of the main news outlets gather for the morning editorial meeting. The Head of the Newsroom, the Director of BBC News, the Head of Multimedia Programs, the Head of Newsgathering, or one of their deputies chairs the meeting. During my fieldwork, the meeting included representatives of the main news programmes and divisions, including: World News Editor, Business News Editor, Video on Demand Editor, Radio Editor, Newsnight Editor, Sports Editor, 24/7 Editor, morning shows' Editor, Six O'clock News and Ten O'clock News Editor, Bush House Editor, Head of Newsgathering, duty lawyer, UGC Hub representative, Asian Network representative (by video conference), Arabic TV representative (by video conference), and Milbank representative (by video conference).

The 9 a.m. meeting provides a venue to discuss editorial issues that affect how the BBC will cover individual stories across its programmes and outputs. The 9 a.m. editorial meeting normally starts with the chair asking each programme editor which stories they will cover that day. During the meeting, the editors discuss the rolling stories of the day and the news angles for each story. The meetings are also a chance to confirm that stories and news angles do not conflict, and to avoid conflicts across BBC programmes and outputs.[10] The news day therefore does not start with a blank sheet. Some events are calendar-driven and topic-driven: For instance, throughout the year journalists monitor large annual events such as Davos, or topics such as corruption. The J-Portal contains lists of yearly events as well as recurrent stories, and provides documentation. Tech-savvy journalists are part of the daily intake of news involving a sequence of meetings.

In January 2011, social media came to BBC journalists' attention during the 9 a.m. meeting. An editor had sent a few journalists to Tunis to cover the uprising. Journalists had several good reasons to use social media in the early stages of the uprising. First, the BBC's newsgathering resources were limited. Journalists used small tourist cameras because protestors smashed Independent Television Network (ITN) cameras. In Tunis, the Internet was also slow and the tools to cover the news were rudimentary and fragile. Second, the news organisation had deployed few journalists and minimal equipment. The situation became increasingly dangerous for journalists when Tunisian officials imposed a curfew on everyone in the capital. In addition, the hotels were full. Because many Tunisians believed that France had prompted the uprising, there was a backlash against the French and those suspected of helping them. For these reasons, editors agreed that it was better to wait until the situation stabilised in Tunis before sending additional journalists. The editors recommended to journalists to use social media to cover the news despite the slow Internet connection in Tunis. Reporters in Tunis mentioned using Facebook, Twitter, and e-mail as tools to contact journalists and gather information to cover events taking place across North Africa and the Middle East. The individual work of traditional and UGC Hub journalists was central in gathering information on these unfolding events. During the morning editorial meeting determining the news agenda, editors made these logistical and editorial decisions, something that we need to account for when analysing news production.

The daily intake does not stop with the 9 a.m. editorial meeting. There are several other important daily and weekly editorial meetings in the news organisation. Daily meetings include the "newsgathering next day deployment", "the pan-news editorial", "rest of the day/evening output", "the pan-news editorial 'next day output'", and the "overnight news meeting". Other meetings throughout the day follow the morning pan-news editorial meeting. For instance, the Six O'clock News and Ten O'clock News unit meets at 11 a.m. every morning. The Six O'clock News and the Ten O'clock News meeting is chaired by the Deputy Editor of the day and attended by the editors and the producers. During the meeting, participants debrief from the previous day and discuss the angles and headlines they plan to use in the day's news. The Deputy Editor provides direction based on what s/he has seen at the morning editorial meeting. S/he sets up the news agenda for the day, keeping in mind that it may be altered as events evolve, and assigns one or more stories to the producers. There are also weekly meetings focused on planning. These meetings include "pan-news planning", "programs planning", and "pan-news commissioning".

When the formal and informal morning meetings end, journalists learn about the day's order of news stories and read the news. For example, some journalists look at hashtags (#) and followers' tweet feeds on Twitter. After lunch, journalists start putting news pieces together. At this time, the work of writing, editing, and sub-editing stories also begins. The producer leads these tasks and is responsible for writing stories and sub-editing segments of the news bulletin. Writing and sub-editing depends on the availability of sources, chosen news angles, logistical capabilities, user-generated content, and editorial decisions. The Duty Editor looks at each producer's written scripts and provides editorial guidance.

The news stories come from several sources of information. For example, the BBC has an internal news agency, the Newswire unit, which is divided into three branches: video on demand (VOD), the UGC Hub, and wire agencies. The Newswire is the main tool providing updated information to journalists. Social media also feed the news production cycle, along with traditional feeds such as news wire agencies. Since 7/7, the UGC Hub has become an essential part of breaking news. The UGC Hub journalists have been soliciting and finding content such as pictures and videos, sources, and stories; monitoring stories and developing news angles; or answering e-mails generated by stories and users' comments. Sylvia Costeloe at the UGC Hub said that "in many instances, the first pictures these days that come out are user generated pictures" (Costeloe quoted in Stray, 2010). The first images from breaking news stories such as the Haiti earthquake in 2010 and the London 7/7 bombings in 2005 originated from social media sources. During these and other breaking news stories, social media are added as an extra dimension to the daily news cycle. This is true even up to the moment before a story goes on the air.

Thirty minutes before news bulletins such as the Six O'clock News and the Ten O'clock News, presenters and producers go to the production room and start rehearsing the show. By starting early, the presenters can re-record the opening or polish some of the pieces of the bulletin. Although the news stories are lined up at this point in the news timeline, producers can still make changes to the bulletin. For instance, during my fieldwork, a picture originating from a social media source was set to appear on the Six O'clock News. At the last minute, the producers removed the picture because the owner of the picture had not granted legal copyright approval. A producer selected another picture for the story.

After the bulletin is aired, the team conducts debriefings and post-mortems. These exercises help journalists wrap up the bulletin and discuss new angles for future bulletins. Debriefings and post-mortems are chaired by the Deputy Editor of the day; s/he talks about the positive and less positive aspects of each news piece presented in the show. Most of the stories are picked up by the Ten O'clock News bulletin. The BBC identifies certain stories as being suited to specific audiences. Physically located between World News and UK News, the online team can pick up existing stories, generate new stories, and publish stories online.

The news production cycle involves timelines for programmes, meetings, organisational structures, physical settings, editorial considerations, and logistics. At the BBC, social media are integrated into the newsgathering process and act as an extra newsgathering tool for programmes and outputs, both on a daily cycle and particularly in breaking news. Although social media are centralised in the UGC Hub, journalists have a role in deciding if it is appropriate to trust social media sources. Journalists can choose, select, and publish the material. The BBC has thus responded to social media by creating centralised structures involving more tech-savvy journalists.

In recent years, news organisations have created new positions such as social media editors. At the BBC, the Social Media Editor's role was created in November 2009 and filled by Alex Gubbay, former Editor for BBC Interactive Sports News (BBC Press Office, 2009). This move demonstrates the increasing role of tech-savvy journalists in the newsroom, helping the BBC to develop ways to collaborate with its audiences. At the same time, the appointment of a Social Media Editor highlights how, with the increasing demand to manage social media, these activities have been centralised in the hands of tech-savvy journalists. These journalists took on the role of coordinating this form of material across the newsroom.

SOCIAL MEDIA EDUCATION

BBC social media management also played a role in the education of tech-savvy journalists. Emerging as an upshot of the Neil Report of 2004, the BBC College of Journalism has been a pillar of journalism and social media education. More than the mere result of institutional decisions and structural constraints, the evolution of social media training at the BBC is the product of socio-technological, politico-economic, and institutional conditions, as well as the ability of certain actors at the public broadcaster to respond strategically to social media in the new media logic. Here we notice the increasing role of tech-savvy journalists in the process.

Social media training has its institutional origins in the Neil Report published in 2004. The Neil Report considered lessons for BBC journalism. The Report was the BBC's reaction to the Hutton inquiry,[11] commissioned by the British government in response to the death of Dr David Kelly.[12]

After the publication of the Hutton Report, BBC Director General Mark Byford commissioned a report from Ron Neil, who at the time was Director of News and Current Affairs, to look at the editorial issues raised by the Hutton inquiry. Byford also asked Neil to "identity the learning lessons and make appropriate recommendations" (Barnett, 2011). The Neil Report recommended a series of reforms, including fostering a well-trained journalistic workforce to improve standards. The Report argued that as the largest employer of journalists in the United Kingdom, the BBC had an obligation to be the leader in strengthening journalistic skills and encouraging debate on journalistic ethics. Further, each programme needed to have the same ethics, values, professional discipline, and culture (BBC, 2005). The BBC governors pledged to implement the Report's recommendations. Mark Thompson asked Mark Byford to quickly implement the Report's recommendations. As a result, the BBC designed special classes for its journalists. The BBC had trained its journalists, but the Report pushed for clarifying certain practices; for example, by offering lessons on reliable note-taking. The Report also called for a new in-house training programme. In 2005, the new BBC launched the College of Journalism:

> Coursework supporting five editorial principles defined in the Neil Report will be done in BBC buildings or close to the workplace, with external training activity supplied through partnerships with training providers. There will also be a significant shift of emphasis in content. In addition to the core journalistic craft and production skills which have been the mainstay of journalist training in recent years, the new College of Journalism will also focus on ethics and values, and building knowledge on key themes and issues, such as Europe and the Middle East. The enhanced training is already underway. So far 10,000 members of staff have completed the online editorial policy course (the biggest BBC interactive training initiative yet) and 8,000 staff have attended special Neil workshops. All journalistic staff in the BBC will be given a minimum level of training each year and in future the completion of required training will be seen as integral to promotion.
>
> (BBC, 2005)

According to Mark Byford, training spending would double from £5 million annually to £10 million by 2008. Training covered world service, nations and regions, and other areas of the BBC. The plan included a virtual college and a new director of training. Each year, journalists would need to attain a minimum level of training that would range from ethics and values to editorial policy. In 2005 there was no specific social media course provided to journalists, because social media were still nascent.

In April 2006, under the leadership of Mark Thompson, the BBC unveiled Creative Future, an editorial endeavour designed to deliver more value to its audiences. Creative Future was a response to the 2006 White Paper on the new BBC Charter (see Chapter 1). In the 2006 White Paper, the BBC redefined its purposes. They included playing a leading role in new technological developments. The White Paper became part of the vision and practices of the BBC. The vision meant:

- Making digital content and services available on a variety of platforms and devices
- Working with the media industry to develop a UK-wide digital television network
- Supporting the coverage of Digital Audio Broadcasting (DAB)
- Supporting the United Kingdom digital switchover in April 2012
- Working with other organisations to sensitise audiences to emerging communication technologies and services
- Supporting the government's help scheme to the most vulnerable groups during the digital switchover

(DCMS, 2006)

The BBC wrote about social media in 2007, in the report titled *From Seesaw to Wagon Wheel: Safeguarding Impartiality in the 21st Century.* That report was the first instance of the BBC discussing social media as part of the organisation's ideal of impartiality. Although new media had been on the agenda for awhile, the publication of *From Seesaw to Wagon Wheel* signalled a new period of integration of social media in BBC journalism.

After a period of trial and error with social media, the BBC launched the BBC Academy in mid-December 2009. The Academy is the centre for training in which the Colleges of Journalism, Production, Leadership, and Technology are based. Originally, from 2005 to 2009, the content available on the College website was available only to the BBC employees. In 2009, the plan for the Academy included: making the BBC College of Journalism website available to anyone in the UK and to subscribers outside the United Kingdom; collaborating with Independent Television (ITV) to improve media industry employability and Channel 4 to ensure diversity; sharing the BBC training model with trade and lobby groups including the Broadcasting, Entertainment, Cinematograph, and Theatre Union (BECTU), the largest broadcasting union in the United Kingdom, and the Producer Alliance for Cinema and Television (PACT), the independent producers' trade body, in order to enhance the public's understanding of BBC capabilities and practices. Social media training at the BBC is thus idiosyncratic. The BBC started providing social media courses to journalists in 2009. According to a BBC College of Journalism trainer, these courses were developed as a reaction to the emergence of social media.[13]

Since 2009, the BBC has held various types of social media training sessions at the BBC Academy and College of Journalism, highlighting the centrality of tech-savvy journalists in social media endeavours. In November 2009, the BBC developed the first social media course called Making the

Web Work for You. The non-mandatory course trained BBC journalists in the manner of using social media, finding user-generated content, and building communities of audience members (Wardle and Williams, 2010). The course was held during one full working day and involved 15 journalists. Making the Web Work for You introduced journalists to Facebook (Wardle and Williams, 2009). It also introduced them to digital tools on the Internet and the use of advanced Google search (Wardle and Williams, 2009). According to BBC trainer Chris Walton, Making the Web Work for You "equipped journalists with the new digital tools they needed to find people, case studies and stories, and it set them up on Twitter and Facebook accounts to source content and interact with our audience" (Walton, 2012). While journalists participated in the course, they put their new knowledge into action by following the class on their laptop. For course trainers, it was important that journalists used the new tools during the learning process.[14]

Several characteristics of Making the Web Work for You show the BBC's social media approach in that early period. First, as illustrated above, the BBC offered social media training to BBC journalists. Second, the BBC's approach to education was hesitant. The courses were given on the basis that there had been a problem that needed to be solved with training. In an interview, BBC College of Journalism's staff stated,

> My boss said to me, 'I want you to do something on social media.' I then investigated and looked around. We hired a freelance person called Claire Wardle, who was a former academic at Cardiff School of Journalism. She developed the content with me overseeing it, but it was mainly her for the content for the courses.[15]

Some older journalists resisted the uses of social media early in the process.

From 2009 to 2010, the BBC held social media courses exclusively for its own journalists. At this early stage of the BBC's training scheme, only non-BBC journalists undertook one-on-one training sessions with BBC journalists. Since 2010 social media have been integrated into media courses within the BBC.[16] For instance, in the fall of 2012, the Academy gave a five-day course for the Journalism Foundation. A half-day was dedicated to discussing ways that journalists can use social media tools in their reporting, newsgathering, and sourcing. The Academy also developed a series of week-long intensive programmes: the New Journalists Programme, the Editorial Leadership Programme, and the Social Media and Digital Journalism Programme.

Each of the courses highlighted the importance of managing and verifying online sources, setting up effective social media tactics while engaging with the audience, directing them back to traditional news content, and promoting BBC editorial values. The Editorial Leadership Programme covers editorial guidance and content. Broadcasters, freelancers, students, and independent media organisations had attended the course. The Social Media and Digital Journalism Programme teaches participants how to find original stories and content online, how to verify, how to filter the "noise" on the Internet, how to set up newsfeeds, how to cope with real time news, how to engage and develop loyalty with an audience, and how to drive that audience to traditional content such as programmes and outputs (online, television, or radio). That year the BBC also launched a UGC Editorial Standards course for editors and independents. That course taught journalists how to verify content; post, share, and engage with the audience; analyse metrics; and evaluate the success rate of social media endeavours. This course focused on how journalists can use social media and how social media can add to traditional news production.

As trainers and techies gained a better understanding of how to use social media, the BBC was able to be more proactive in incorporating new media into BBC newsgathering. BBC journalists also worked with industry leaders and academics to define social media practices and journalism. During the Arab Spring in 2011, many journalists realised the value of using social media in their daily work (see also Doucet, 2011). Post-Arab Spring, the BBC started providing additional one-on-one training sessions and created a forum for BBC journalists, independent media producers, and social media organisations. For example, in May 2011, the BBC held its first BBC Social Media Summit (#bbcsms) where participants discussed transformation in journalistic innovations, values, norms, editorial standards, and practices. The summit has been held every year since.

Organised by Claire Wardle and BBC College of Journalism trainers, the summit was designed to gather industry leaders and scholars of journalism to discuss the development of social media in journalism (Eltringham, 2011). It discussed how journalists could best use social media in their daily work. The BBC made the proceedings available on Twitter, blog articles, and videos on the College of Journalism blog and the BBC's YouTube channel. The first day's discussions targeted representatives of news organisations and followed the Chatham House Rule, a principle that allows participants to share the information that they receive but requires that they not reveal the identity or affiliation of speakers or other participants. At the summit, one of the journalists asked, "how have national and international news organisations incorporated social media in their reporting and their newsrooms?" (Eltringham, 2011).

The second day of the conference took place at the BBC campus in White City (in the building at the end of Woodlane), open to about 150 journalists each session. I attended the activities that day. The conference included questions involving verification, ethics, cultural changes, editorial issues, audience expectations, and news coverage. For example, Peter Horrocks argued that the broadcaster's approach has

> Got to be carrots and sticks. It has to start with a clear vision of what we are trying to achieve as news organisations. . . . We have got to

change things. You can't assume this is all fixed. People who are more conservative and less willing to move rapidly will respond really badly to that kind of extremism. It has got to be a coalition of interests.

(fieldnotes, 2011)

Other journalists and social media players took part in the debate. For example, Liz Heron of *The New York Times* discussed humanising social media practices, for example by personalising tweets. She stated that at *The New York Times*, Twitter is "a fully human experience without the auto-mated headlines being pumped through it". In a video, NPR's Andy Carvin discussed how he curated content on Twitter during the Arab Spring. Other social media specialists such as Esra Dogramaci, Social Media Coordinator from Al Jazeera Turkish, said that to distil social media content, journal-ists need to follow the following equation: Information—noise + context = responsible reporting. A BBC journalist in the audience challenged Esra, saying that Al Jazeera journalism facilitated revolution by providing cam-eras to citizens. In his closing address Alan Rusbridger, Editor in Chief of *The Guardian*, said, "People working in this generation of journalism just have to accept . . . open media is better than closed media". At the confer-ence, BBC journalists, academics, and social media professionals explored what are the best practices of social media. BBC journalists took stands on what they thought were the social media best practices, such as during the conversation between Esra Dogramaci and the BBC journalist.

Since 2011, the BBC has offered different types of "how to" social media courses: editorial (Social Media Overview for editors and executives who wanted to know what they need to put in place to have social media accounts) and practical (Twitter Basic, Twitter Advanced, Facebook for Pro-ducers, Social Media Best Practice, Social Media and Connected Journalism, and Making the Web Work for You). The BBC also offered an Internet source course, which consists of an introduction to social media tools and LinkedIn to find material and case study. The Academy also offered the sem-inar "New Social Media Tools" to journalists who wanted to learn about Twitter and Facebook's uses and shortcomings (Sharma, 2012). Addition-ally, the BBC Academy gave a five-day intensive course entitled Social Media and Digital Journalism Programme, as well as the Editorial Leadership Pro-gramme. Initially, the BBC provided these courses to teach social media understanding and strategy to its journalists. Subsequently, these courses provided lessons to individual reporters and news organisations around the world, not just to BBC journalists. The BBC also recommended that jour-nalists take a five-day intensive BBC New Journalist Programme course. That course integrated social media into discussions of story finding, sto-rytelling, multimedia practices, ethics and values, and understanding audi-ences. Training specialists, including Claire Wardle, Sue Llewellyn, Ramaa Sharma, and Marc Blank-Settle, led these training sessions. Since 2012, the BBC has offered social media consulting that goes beyond the boundaries of the news organisation. As a BBC College of Journalism instructor stated, "If a radio station in Cambridge wants media training, we may have a couple of options. They'll run some formal training course in the classroom but there's a lot of one-to-one. We have a training model, it's not just classroom training".[17]

In these efforts, the BBC sought to portray itself as the mediator of the media industry, using social media training as a tool. According to Chris Walton, since 2009, "the BBC has also put in place an effective social media training programme, bringing thousands of our journalists up to speed and ensuring they are comfortable with handling the new material and the new social spaces" (Walton, 2012).

Since 2009, the BBC has used the BBC Academy in its strategy to become a leader of social media training in quality journalism. As of 2012, more than 3,000 BBC News staff had received training on Twitter, Facebook, LinkedIn, or Flickr, in groups or one-on-one sessions (Walton, 2012). The BBC has also become more forward-looking by using smart phones for newsgathering and distribution of news.[18] For instance, the BBC College of Journalism has trained more than 400 journalists inside and outside the United Kingdom on how to use smart phones (Settle-Blank, 2012). These can do the job of a laptop, an audio recorder, a still camera, a video camera, a television, and a radio. Martin Turner, BBC Head of Operations, Newsgathering, wrote in a blog post that "many BBC staff with an iPhone will soon get a bespoke app to enable material to be filed directly into content production systems" (Turner in Settle-Blank, 2012). Training tips for smart phones range from holding the phone with both hands to using apps to facilitate searches or take better pictures. With hindsight, social media education is another example of how social media has gained significance within the BBC's traditional journalism. At the same time, we see new actors (tech-savvy journalists) taking leadership roles within the organisation.

NEW GUIDELINES

Tech-savvy journalists have quickly gained significance at the BBC. These new actors gained power in the management of social media in the newsroom. At the same time as the BBC took steps to manage social media, it also launched the BBC social networking guidelines in March 2008. Kevin Bakhurst, former Deputy Head of the Newsroom, attested, "[l]ike many established news providers, we have created an open and modern set of guidances to help our staff engage, gather news and spread their journalism, working within the BBC's editorial values that are at the core of our journalism" (Bakhurst, 2011). Similarly, Helen Boaden stated, "the new guidelines about what content BBC staff could put on social networking websites were designed to protect the corporation's brand" (Boaden paraphrased in Sweney, 2008b).

The BBC social networking guidelines[19] were sent to BBC staff in early 2008.[20] The Corporation encouraged its journalists to add context when using social media. For instance, the guidelines stated, "add your own comment to the 'tweet' you have selected, making it clear why you are forwarding it, when you are speaking in your own voice and when you are quoting someone else's" (BBC Social Networking Guidelines, 2008). The guidelines took into account issues of privacy. For example, they prohibit journalists from using pictures they find on social media without gaining permission from the copyright owner. Helen Boaden said that the public and private space remains complicated. Indeed, many citizens are not aware when they publish pictures that such images can be used in the media (Boaden in Sweney, 2008b). Social media quickly gained significance in the newsroom, but that social media was managed centrally in the hands of tech-savvy journalists.

TECH-SAVVY JOURNALISTS RE-DEFINING REPORTING

The BBC has allowed a more prominent space for these journalists to work within the newsroom and integrate social media into their daily professional activities and BBC organisational structures. Certain features of the media logic have led to the gain of power of a new generation of tech-savvy journalists in the newsroom, who arrived in the newsroom in greater numbers in the 1990s. The conditions leading to this new generation can be grouped under three main categories: political-economic, institutional and organisational, and socio-technological. The conditions are also "part of the broader media ecosystem and as a profession that has its own unique ways of dealing with such influences" (Deuze, 2008):

> First, political-economic conditions have led to the increase in presence and power of tech-savvy journalists in the newsroom. These conditions included cuts in the BBC's budget and, as a result, the centralisation (in 2007–08) of the UGC Hub in the middle of the multimedia newsroom from its former home on the 7th floor of the Television Centre. During this period, the BBC undertook a series of actions to reduce the costs of news production material to cover news events. This cost-reduction effort led to increased use of the free material the BBC sought and received from its audiences.
> (see also Chouliaraki, 2010b; Bruns, 2008; Turner, 2010)

Second, institutionally, tech-savvy journalists have acquired more influence in the newsroom. For example, the 2004 Neil Report led to the creation of the BBC College of Journalism. Today, the College of Journalism is home to dedicated journalist-trainers teaching social media to journalists, managers, and other staff of the BBC. The official launch of the UGC Hub in 2005, the creation of the Social Media Editor in 2008 and official social media representatives across the newsroom, the integration of UGC Hub staff in editorial and planning meetings, as well as the integration of social media in the J-Portal, outputs, and programmes, all suggest growth, in numbers and in significance, of techies in the newsroom.

Third, socio-technological conditions have led to the revival of power of techies in the BBC newsroom and a need to manage social media. In a short period of time, social media have gained significance in the newsroom (Jones and Salter, 2012). The creation of new structures—paired with politico-economic, institutional, and socio-technological conditions—coincide with transformations in journalistic norms and practices geared toward more collaborative crisis reporting, in which the BBC has bolstered its vision.

NOTES

1. The BBC's Global News division, under the leadership of Peter Horrocks at the time of my fieldwork, deals with international newsgathering, which is the main focus of this research project. That division includes the following subdivisions: Controller Digital Technologies; BBC World News/Business Director; BBC international; online news services in English; Controller English Languages (editorial planning); Controller Languages; Finances; Strategy; Government Relations; Legal and Compliance; Human Relations; Public Affairs; BBC Monitoring Service; and BBC World Service Trust, the philanthropic unit of the BBC.
   Source: BBC Global News, 2011
   Managed by the BBC Global News Editor, the international Newsgathering team is spread worldwide and includes 82 overseas bureaux, journalists, stringers, London-based correspondents, and producers in BBC World Service and Television Centre. In contrast to BBC UK, which is domestically oriented, BBC World News is responsible for managing the overseas bureaux, World News Planning, World Affairs unit, World Newsdesk, World News Special Events, World TV reporters, and Radio. The BBC World Newsgathering unit counts among its staff the World News Editor and the World Assignment editor. In 2011, these two editors were located in the Television Centre in White City and Bush House on Aldwich in Central London. In 2012, the UK Foreign Office stopped financing the World Service and sold Bush House. Bush House's (BBC World Service) financial source is the licence fees' budget. During my fieldwork the unit ran overseas bureaux ("hubs") in seven world regions: Africa (Johannesburg), Americas (Washington), Asia (Beijing), Europe (Brussels), former Soviet Union (Moscow), Middle East (Jerusalem), and South Asia (Delhi). There are reporters, including freelance and unsponsored reporters, located across international hubs. Along with that, the UGC Hub sought and received material from unpaid, "ordinary" citizen witnessing events. Within the Newsgathering unit, the Newsgathering operations and its Head of Operations provide the staff and technologies to cover the deployment of logistics and facilities. The team covers the assignments in the UK and internationally. The Resource and Development team responsible for the management of newsgathering resources manages the bureaux. They manage shoot and edit crews, editing, fibre optic circuits, and satellite transponders.

Teams in finance, human resources, and occupational health support the Newsgathering team located in the London multimedia newsroom.

2. Notes on the general structure of the BBC multimedia newsroom: In the early years of the BBC, the organisation was ordered around functions rather than personalities (Briggs, 1985, 147–148). After the Second World War, the general structure was distributed across regions, following the recommendation of the Beveridge Report. In the 1990s, the Director General became increasingly central in determining the level of the licence fee (Barnett and Curry, 1994). The BBC News Group is situated under the Director General's office and the BBC Direction Group (BDG), which are jointly responsible for managing the whole Corporation. During my fieldwork, the BBC general structure was divided in seven sections: BBC Vision; BBC Finance & Business; Audio & Music; Future Media; Operations; BBC North; and News Group. Announced on 14 February 2013, and applied from Tuesday, 2 April 2013, the BBC Management Group replaced the BBC Direction Group for managing pan-BBC issues and meeting its objectives. This group is delegated from the Executive Board and meets three times a month. The members of the Board include: Tony Hall (Director General), Roger Mosey (Acting Director, Television), Francesca Unsworth (Acting Director, News), Helen Boaden (Director, Radio), James Purnell (Director, Strategy & Digital), Zarin Patel (Chief Financial Officer), Lucy Adams (Director, HR), Peter Salmon (Director, North), Ken MacQuarrie (Director, Scotland), Rhodri Talfan-Davies (Director, Wales), Peter Johnston (Director, Northern Ireland), David Jordan (Director, Editorial Policy & Standards), Ralph Rivera (Director, Future Media), Philip Almond (Director, Marketing), Alan Yentob (Creative Director), Tim Davie (Chief Executive Officer, BBC Worldwide & Director, Global). The BBC structure now separates the day-to-day working into eight areas: the Director General's Office and Management Board, Radio, BBC North, Finance and Business, Future Media, News Group, and Television. The BBC has three commercial subsidiaries: BBC Worldwide, BBC Studios and Post-Production, and BBC World News. The Corporation is established by the Royal Charter, the BBC Trust governs it, the Executive Board is responsible for its operation. And media regulators, Ofcom and the UK Department for Culture, Media, and Sport (DCMS), regulate its activities (BBC, 2013c). Overseen by the Director General's Office, that was led by Mark Thompson during my fieldwork, and the BBC Direction Group, the BBC News Group includes three divisions. Each of these divisions has its own social media strategy. These divisions are: BBC News, the unit responsible for organising newsgathering activities; BBC English Regions; and BBC Global News. These three divisions are responsible for the BBC's news, current affairs, and sports outputs. The BBC News Group included the following positions during my fieldwork: Director, Controller of Production; Controller, Strategy, News and Audio & Music; Head of Newsroom; Controller English Regions; Director Global News; Head of Political Programmes and Analysis; Director BBC Northern Ireland; Director BBC Scotland; Deputy Director of News and Head of News Programmes; Director BBC Cymru Wales; Director Human Resources; and Director Newsgathering. In 2013, the following positions were included in the BBC News Group: Director of News and Current Affairs; Deputy Director of News and Current Affairs; Director of Global News; Head of Political Programmes; Head of Multimedia Newsroom; Finance Director of News; Human Resources Director; News Group and Radio; Director of Marketing and Audiences of News; Controller, Strategy of News and Radio; Controller of English Regions; Controller of Production of News; Controller of English

of BBC Global News; Controller of Languages of BBC Global News (BBC, 2013b).

3. 24/7 News Editor, interview 2011.
4. Senior Manager, interview 2011.
5. 24/7 News Editor, interview 2011.
6. World Service Social Media Manager, interview 2011.
7. The White Paper of BBC Journalism Portal is available here: www.bbc.co.uk/blogs/legacy/bbcinternet/img/bbc_journalism_portal_white_paper.pdf.
8. Online News Editor Wales, interview 2011.
9. Fieldwork notes, 2011.
10. Assistant Editor, multimedia newsroom, interview 2011.
11. On 24 September 2002, the UK government published a dossier entitled *Iraq Weapons of Mass Destruction: The Assessment of the British Government.* On 22 May 2003, BBC journalist Andrew Gilligan met with Dr David Kelly, an expert in biological weapons at the British Ministry of Defence, and a former United Nations inspector of weapons in Iraq. Following the meeting, on 29 May 2003, Gilligan broadcasted a report on the Today programme on BBC Radio 4. The BBC reporter alleged that the Blair government had "sexed up" the dossier. Gilligan named Dr Kelly as a source. Following this, Kelly was called before the parliamentary foreign affairs select committee and heavily questioned. On 18 July 2003, two days after meetings with Gilligan, the hearing at the House of Commons, and the resulting BBC news reports, Kelly was found dead from suicide at his home in Oxfordshire. Following this series of events, the British government asked Lord Hutton to "investigate the circumstances surrounding the death of Dr Kelly" (Hutton, 2004, 2). The government accused the BBC of breach in impartiality and, as a consequence, the inquiry asked strenuous questions about the ability of the BBC to remain impartial. The inquiry resulted in the resignation of both General Manager Greg Dyke and Chairperson of the Board of Governors Gavyn Davies (Dyke in BBC, 2004b). A group of BBC journalists subsequently walked out of the BBC Broadcasting House and offices around the UK including Cardiff, Glasgow, and Newcastle, and protested against Dyke's resignation. On 31 January 2004, a group of journalists paid for a full-page advertisement in *The Daily Telegraph* to express their anger at Dyke's resignation. More than 4,000 journalists signed the statement (Dyke, 2004).
12. In 2004, during the Hutton inquiry, the British government questioned whether the BBC could be impartial. According to former BBC General Manager Mark Thompson, the inquiry was the "biggest crisis in BBC journalism" and raised questions about the future of impartiality (Thompson in Douglas, 2004). The inquiry and General Manager Greg Dyke's departure from the BBC affected the culture of the organisation by encouraging a more risk-averse approach to journalism. Shaken by the Hutton inquiry, the BBC commissioned an internal report called the Neil Report building on lessons learned from Hutton, and suggesting initiatives that the BBC should undertake to protect its impartiality and independence. Acting Director General Mark Byford, following Dyke's dramatic resignation during the inquiry, summoned the panel. Ronald Neil chaired the Report and the review team included Helen Boaden, Controller of BBC Radio 4; Richard Tait, former ITN Editor in Chief; Glenwyn Benson, Controller Factual Commissioning Television; Adrian Van Klaveren, Head of BBC Newsgathering; and Stephen Whittle, Controller BBC Editorial Policy. As in 1949, the Report defined BBC journalism as balanced, un-opinionated, and fair. It described BBC journalism as accurate, robust, independent, and impartial. It inspired several changes at the BBC which pointed towards more "open" and "collaborative" forms of journalism. For example, it promoted

improved training and standards by creating the BBC College of Journalism, which now offers social media courses. It also recommended that the BBC reform how it manages audience complaints. Social media as a keyword were still absent from the language employed at the time of the Report. Yet the Neil Report illustrates the general trend of the BBC to collaborate more with its audience.

13. BBC College of Journalism staff, interview 2012.
14. BBC College of Journalism staff, interview 2012.
15. BBC College of Journalism staff, interview 2012.
16. BBC College of Journalism staff, interview 2012.
17. BBC College of Journalism staff, interview 2012.
18. Marc Blank-Settle, BBC College of Journalism, e-mail exchange 2012.
19. The BBC asked the journalists to be mindful that the information they could disclose should protect the reputation of the organisation. Within this axis, concerns over the idea of impartiality were brought up in the guidelines: "when forwarding or 're-tweeting' messages, care should be taken that it does not appear that the BBC is endorsing a particular opinion".
20. Four commandments directed the guidelines in social media dealings: (1) engage in conversations and online conversations, (2) do not put the BBC into disrepute, (3) trust users, and (4) be open and transparent (BBC Social Networking Guidelines, 2008).

5   The Connected Newsroom[1]

As new technologies of communication and surveillance proliferate, so images of disaster around the world pervade everyday life, and bearing witness becomes increasingly mediated.

(Pantti, Wahl-Jorgensen, and Cottle, 2012,178)

SOCIAL NETWORKING AND ITS IMPACT ON BBC CRISIS REPORTING

In this book, I have explored how journalists use social media to produce and disseminate news content. I have looked into the redefinition of journalistic norms and practices such as impartiality and verification. I have also focused on how BBC journalists observe, shape, and articulate new technologies in their daily practices. Since the London bombing attacks on 7 July 2005, the scale and the extent to which journalists have used social media in crisis reporting have increased exponentially. Since 7/7, social media have changed BBC journalistic practices and norms, structures of the newsroom, and discourse regarding reporting of crisis events. BBC journalists have learned to use Twitter, Facebook, and other social networks to report stories such as the 2008 Mumbai attacks, the 2009 Iranian Elections, and the 2011 Tunisian uprisings. The emergence of social media in news production has thus influenced the nature and representation in the news of global crisis reporting. Since the London bombing attacks of 2005, BBC journalism has experienced substantial transformations. And the incorporation of social media into BBC journalism has been crafted around existing journalistic practices and norms.

This book has revealed the contradictory and uneven nature of news production, and the tensions between old and new media at the BBC via journalistic uses of social media in crisis reporting. Impartiality at the BBC now reveals openness and transparency. Journalists have also become curators of information online. The BBC institutionalised new professional roles, including the Social Media Editor and social media trainers specialising in smartphones.

This book has also shown that the incorporation of social media into BBC crisis reporting represents a transformation in norms and practices that is part of a larger cultural and institutional shift of the BBC's relationship with its audiences and its presentation of crisis reporting. For example, citizens' increasing use of social media in crisis reporting led to a need to manage social media material within the organisation (Bennett, 2013; Chouliaraki, 2010; Harrisson, 2009). In that context, the role of BBC tech-savvy journalists in managing user-generated content became even more relevant. As a result, new structures accommodating the new media logic have supplanted the structures that existed in the media logic that predated the emergence of social media.

Technological, political, cultural, and organisational forces have affected how BBC news is produced and presented. For instance, changes in journalistic uses of social networks coincide with BBC changes in policy, including the 2008 Statement Programme Policy. In that book, the BBC delineated a plan to make user-generated content part of the BBC News proposition across its platforms by creating technical infrastructure and editorial and managerial processes for journalists to work closely with audiences.

Correspondingly, tensions between old and new journalistic traditions and changing power relations in news production and media systems have altered the news discourse: The BBC now produces a more networked and connected journalism in crisis reporting. The incorporation of audiences in news production is not new, but the Internet and social networks have allowed crisis reporting to become more collaborative and less paternalistic. The outlook of the first Director General of the BBC, John Reith, who had little trust in the ability of the public to select remarkable information in order to take part in public debates, had evolved considerably. In other words, this transformation in the way the public broadcaster selects, organises, and disseminates the news reflects a wider shift toward a networked information economy that offers a reorganisation of the public sphere (Benkler, 2006, 465).

The transformation in journalistic norms and practices at the British public broadcaster occurs within the media logic. Integrating the journalistic developments into the media logic framework clarifies how the changes and challenges of today's news industry affect (or refrain from affecting) the professional routines of journalists (Deuze, 2008). The media logic framework means that journalists use professional ethical codes that are specific to their profession, including accuracy, impartiality, verification, and balance, to sustain their journalistic independence. These codes are, in turn, articulated in the new technological communication infrastructure (involving social media), which allows people in the logic to interact and leads to new power relations in the media logic and the news.[2]

This chapter reflects on the extent to which social media have transformed BBC journalism—its norms, practices, and discourse—and relations between the BBC and its audiences in crisis reporting. This chapter also

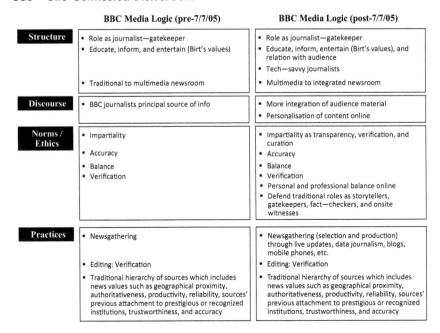

	BBC Media Logic (pre-7/7/05)	BBC Media Logic (post-7/7/05)
Structure	• Role as journalist—gatekeeper • Educate, inform, and entertain (Birt's values) • Traditional to multimedia newsroom	• Role as journalist—gatekeeper • Educate, inform, entertain (Birt's values), and relation with audience • Tech—savvy journalists • Multimedia to integrated newsroom
Discourse	• BBC journalists principal source of info	• More integration of audience material • Personalisation of content online
Norms / Ethics	• Impartiality • Accuracy • Balance • Verification	• Impartiality as transparency, verification, and curation • Accuracy • Balance • Verification • Personal and professional balance online • Defend traditional roles as storytellers, gatekeepers, fact—checkers, and onsite witnesses
Practices	• Newsgathering • Editing: Verification • Traditional hierarchy of sources which includes news values such as geographical proximity, authoritativeness, productivity, reliability, sources' previous attachment to prestigious or recognized institutions, trustworthiness, and accuracy	• Newsgathering (selection and production) through live updates, data journalism, blogs, mobile phones, etc. • Editing: Verification • Traditional hierarchy of sources which includes news values such as geographical proximity, authoritativeness, productivity, reliability, sources' previous attachment to prestigious or recognized institutions, trustworthiness, and accuracy

Figure 5.1   Social Media at BBC News

reflects on how these transformations reveal broader issues of journalistic culture, media institutions, and technologies.

OLD AND NEW FEATURES OF JOURNALISTIC PRACTICES AND NORMS

Tensions and mediation between old and new journalistic features are at the heart of this book. There are several important points of tension and mediation that are worth noting: how social media have enabled journalists to maintain old norms and practices in crisis reporting; how social media have been prominent in stories where journalists have had difficulty bearing witness; how journalists managed their professional and personal balance online; how the transformation of newsgathering and sourcing suggests a continuation of a traditional news values hierarchy; how journalists defend their traditional roles as storytellers, gatekeepers, fact checkers, and onsite witnesses in the new media logic; how, at various points when BBC values were under pressure, journalists took the situation as an opportunity to reaffirm the BBC's editorial procedures and rigour; and how the incorporation of social media in BBC journalism has allowed for the continuation of existing journalistic practices and norms, including impartiality.

Social media have enabled journalists to reaffirm old norms and practices in a network society in which the BBC participates in crisis reporting. Journalistic uses of social media allow for new forms of communication to emerge; these include data journalism and live updates online. Data journalism refers to gathering a mass of information from audiences, interrogating data, and visualising data with online tools such as ManyEyes and Ushahidi (Bradshaw, 2010).[3] Other forms of journalism include BBC live update pages, such as during the news coverage of the Mumbai attacks on the BBC website in 2008. During the Mumbai attacks, the BBC also set up pages on Wikipedia and Google Maps, collaborating with its audiences by showing the locations of the attacks, and linking to news stories and citizen reporting of the unfolding events. Online curating by journalists has also become a more important feature of BBC journalism, particularly with the User-Generated Content Hub and the BBC's live update pages, where evolving news stories are now curated. For example, in an interview, a UGC Hub journalist recognised the authoritative role of the UGC as curator: "There is still a trusted brand to guide people through . . . 'this is good, this is not good.' That is the role of the BBC journalism. Hopefully it will make journalism more interesting on a personal level".[4] This vision is linked to the vision of Reith, but reflects wider preoccupations of public broadcasters and the practice of journalism.

A growing number of curators are developing tools to select social media content. For example, during the 2012 Russian elections, BBC journalists selected preapproved groups, keywords, shared websites, and active users (Vissens, 2012). At the BBC and in other major newsrooms that conduct crisis reporting, social media provide new channels for cultures and extend old media practices and rituals (Bennett, 2012; Chouliaraki, 2010; Hermida, 2012; Hjorth and Kim, 2011, 552; Russell, 2011).

Social media have also been prominent in stories where journalists have had difficulty covering events and tried to "learn from on-the-ground sources" (Lotan et al., 2011, 1376; see also Costeloe in Stray, 2010). For example, the tweets of Sohaib Athar disclosing U.S. special forces' killing of Osama bin Laden in Abbottabad, Pakistan proved to be a primary source of information in the development of the story for the BBC. During the Iranian presidential election in 2009, blogs, Twitter feeds, and YouTube videos in Iran also enabled BBC Persian TV (in Farsi) to report the news.

Citizens now collaborate in news production in selection and production of information via live pages, blogs, comments, forums, user-generated content, social networking, and crowdsourcing. These journalistic practices allow for greater multi-mediality in the narrative structure of journalism by putting citizen eyewitnesses next to journalists reporting online (Chouliaraki, 2010b). Yet foreign correspondents replicate the traditional hierarchy of sources, which includes news values, such as geographical proximity, authoritativeness, past suitability, productivity, reliability, sources' previous attachment to prestigious or recognised institutions, trustworthiness, and accuracy (Galtung and Ruge, 1965). The fact that it is harder for non-institutional organisations or individuals to gain influence on the web partly explains why legacy news journalists replicate the traditional hierarchy of sources (Lasorsa, Lewis, and Holton, 2012).

In a world where citizens increasingly contribute to crisis reporting, the BBC has retained its dominance over collaborative reporting. Nicola Bruno's (2011) finding of the Haiti earthquake reporting confirms that journalists used social media sources minimally in the overall reporting of the earthquake. Bruno added that sources considered reliable and legitimate by BBC reporters, such as well-known non-governmental organisations (NGOs), were most prominent in online pieces about the Haiti earthquake. Even though the public broadcaster retains its dominance over the reporting of crisis events, the presence of social media in crisis reporting should not be underestimated. According to Kevin Bakhurst, former Deputy Head of the BBC Newsroom, now Managing Director of News and Current Affairs at the Irish State Broadcaster RTE,[5] the UGC Hub allowed the BBC to "fully engage in using this material and reinforce the BBC values that our audience expects, in particular accuracy" (Bakhurst, 2011). Bakhurst's guiding vision shows that in the history of the BBC, when its values were under strain, the Corporation took advantage of such opportunities to reinforce its editorial procedures and rigour.

In addition to providing new ways of reporting crises, journalists deal with their professional identity online, particularly in terms of balancing their professional and personal identity (Hermida, 2012, 323). Whereas journalists use social media to gather, filter, report, and disseminate news, they also engage with audiences, talk to colleagues, and make observations about their daily lives. The BBC Editorial Guidelines provide rules for official and unofficial social media accounts, and thus enable journalists to manage a symbolic distinction between their professional and personal lives; of course, whether they follow the rules is another story. In my interviews, journalists emphasised the importance of personalising their social media activities. Most of the social media uses reported by BBC journalists remain on professional accounts. Reflecting this trend, when in 2008 the BBC updated its Guidances to incorporate "social networking", David Jordan, BBC Director for Editorial Policy & Standards, wrote on the BBC Internet Blog to describe a new set of rules for journalists. That new policy drew on "existing BBC policy on conflict of interest which aims to ensure that our journalistic integrity is not compromised by the off-air activities of our presenters and editorial staff" (Jordan, 2008). "It does not restrict BBC staff from conducting legitimate activities on the Internet. It does raise awareness of how crucial the BBC's reputation for impartiality and objectivity is", added Jordan (2008).

Journalists also defend their traditional roles as storytellers, gatekeepers, fact checkers, and onsite witnesses in the media logic. For instance, on 13 January 2010, during the Haiti earthquake news coverage, James Morgan, a broadcast journalist at the BBC, got in touch with the Haitian radio host Carel Pedre on Twitter and authenticated the radio host using BBC verification practices before introducing Pedre to BBC journalists. In another example, during the protests in Tunisia in January 2011, BBC News's Matthew Eltringham verified a tweet by National Public Radio's Andy Carvin and promoted the value of quality journalism and public service broadcasting on Twitter. Eltringham used the BBC Monitoring team's newsgathering expertise to verify the content and found that Carvin's tweet contained false information. Matthew Eltringham defended the fact-checking role of the public broadcaster. Journalists also use traditional journalistic practices such as speaking to the source to ask the 5W questions—who, what, where, why, when, how—and conducting background checks to verify individuals. The UGC Hub's journalists consult experts on date verification to search for the original source of upload and sequences (Murray, 2011). As another example, following the 2012 BBC Trust report on the Arab Spring, on 6 August 2013, the BBC Trust released a follow-up report stating that it now alerts its audience when journalists have not been able to verify pictures or video clips taken by citizens. "Since the review was published, the BBC has adopted new wording for all user-generated footage where independent verification has not been possible and the trust considers this will help the audience understand the vetting process to which all such content is subjected" (BBC Trust, 2013, 2). On Twitter, BBC Social Media Editor Chris Hamilton wrote, "For clarity: BBC doesn't use on-air cautions for *all* UGC material, only if not independently verified www.theguardian.com/media/2013/aug/06/bbc-cautions-user-generated-content". Examples such as these are numerous and continue to increase at the time of this book's publication. These practices are tied to the reliability and accuracy of BBC journalism, a broadcaster that produces quality journalism and delivers value to its audience in times of crisis reporting.

These practices also shed light on the "boundary maintenance" strategy of journalism conceptualised by media scholars (see Lewis, 2012; Usher, 2012; Waisbord, 2013). Boundary maintenance means that journalists maintain distinctions between themselves and other groups. For example, journalists could welcome new practices while bolstering traditional journalism practices and norms, and increase their control over the work process and news output (Cottle and Ashton, 1999, 32). The tension between "old" and "new" approaches was thrust into public view during the Mumbai attacks, when the BBC added an inaccurate tweet to its live page. In a similarly public fashion, the BBC responded to this inaccuracy: After the event, the organisation took the opportunity to enhance accuracy and impartiality by improving methods of verification, contextualisation, and openness on social networks. The BBC's new guidelines emphasised that journalists should treat content from Twitter with the same caution as user-generated content. In the same vein, in 2012, the BBC released new Twitter guidelines asking journalists to go through an editorial process before sending tweets, to minimise the risk of inaccurate or incorrect stories (Hamilton, 2012b).

Several existing journalistic practices and norms have shaped the incorporation of social media into BBC journalism. These have included verification, accuracy, impartiality, and reliability of sources (see Robinson, 2007; 2010; 2011; Ryfe, 2012). Social media have not eradicated traditional journalistic practices. Indeed, most journalists I interviewed emphasised—even romanticised—traditional journalistic practices. For instance, in an interview, a female foreign correspondent pointed out that "there is no substitute for having face to face contact, seeing things. It is very important for a reporter. You can spend a lot of time on the phone or the Internet, but you can't find big pictures and leads. As a reporter, you need personal contacts with people".[6] As another example, BBC journalists contacted social media users such as Athar by phone and by e-mail. By combining new approaches with old principles, the public broadcaster is able to retain its institutional and cultural significance in the new media logic.

NEW RELATIONSHIPS, NEW ROLES

Importantly—and unexpectedly—the increasing use of social media in BBC journalism acted as a catalyst for the increase in power of tech-savvy journalists in the newsroom. With the emergence of social media and the ability of ordinary citizens to take part in news production and dissemination post-7/7, the BBC's need to seek, organise, and curate user-generated content in crisis reporting has grown dramatically in recent years. The demand to manage social media material and the development of new structures in the newsroom allowed for the surge in power of tech-savvy journalists at the BBC. The gain in power of this breed of journalist needs to be understood within the larger political, economic, and cultural changes occurring at the BBC during this period. The BBC's reconstruction of its journalism in crisis reporting is the result of a large-scale organisational effort to become closer to its audiences.

With the arrival of social media in BBC journalism, tech-savvy journalists have enjoyed heightened significance in the newsroom. Since 2005, journalists working at the UGC Hub desk have centrally verified user-generated content and redistributed that material to BBC programmes around the clock. The BBC UGC Hub has acted as consolidator by processing digital videos and images, mobile text messages, blogging content, message boards, e-mails, audio material generated by the audience, and other social media-related activities. According to BBC journalists, these practices have reduced the cost of materials to cover news events. Since 2009, the UGC Hub has assigned a full-time staff member to search for potential news stories and contacts. In November 2009, the BBC appointed Alex Gubbay as the first Social Media Editor. In 2011, when Gubbay left his position as Social Media Editor, the BBC appointed Chris Hamilton.

In response to high demand from journalists seeking social media training, journalists working at the BBC College of Journalism have also developed a series of social media courses for BBC journalists and journalists from other news organisations. The emergence of social media within the context of the 2004 Neil Report's dedication to truth, accuracy, public interest, diversity of opinion, accountability, and independence from the state and commercial interests ushered in these courses.

Since then the BBC has strived to become closer to its audiences and be at the forefront of technological developments in the United Kingdom. It also responded to the emergence of social media that created a need for structures to manage this new and abundant user-generated content. This multifaceted transformation is closely associated with the BBC's "martini media approach", meaning BBC on demand "anytime, anyplace, anywhere". The BBC martini media approach has significantly altered journalists' working environments and identity. This will have implications on the shape public broadcasting journalism will take in the coming years, as the broadcaster finds that social media are an increasingly important source of collaboration with audience, content, and dissemination of news. Tech-savvy journalists are a good point of reference to explore and understand the emerging culture of journalism in a digital age. This will happen as they are taking on increasingly significant roles at the BBC.

The BBC's need to manage social media material and the development of new structures in the newsroom have allowed for the revival of a new breed of tech-savvy journalists in the newsroom. Tech-savvy journalists or other journalists do not lack agency in shaping the structure or taking leadership roles. Structures do not dictate journalists' behaviour. The formation of these structures and the growing volume of social media material coincide with tech-savvy journalists' rise in number and power in the newsroom. Meanwhile, journalists working on the digital side of the newsroom have had the ability and resources to develop guidelines on how to use social media within the practices, norms, and values of BBC journalism. Tech-savvy journalists have been at the forefront of new media changes in the newsroom, such as by providing social media courses to journalists on how to manage social media. These journalists also have joined in the traditional structures that determine the news agenda, including the 9 a.m. morning editorial meeting in the multimedia newsroom.

Tech-savvy journalists have gained influence in the newsroom by their presence within the newsroom and the activities that they have generated. These techies did not appear with the emergence of social media. On the contrary, techies such as Vicky Taylor and Matthew Eltringham were part of BBC News Interactive, from which the UGC Hub emerged. They were already part of the structure and culture of the Corporation. The ascent of the new generation of tech-savvy journalists at the BBC suggests that beyond being normalised in journalistic norms and practices, social media have become part of the fast-changing media logic.

This transformation of the newsroom is not the result of a fluke; the effect of social media in BBC crisis reporting and the Corporation-audience relationship should be understood within the political, economic, cultural, technological, and institutional shift occurring at the BBC, particularly in the aftermath of the 2004 Neil Report. The BBC's re-making of crisis reporting is in large part the result of an organisational effort to become closer to its audiences. The period since the London bombing attacks of July 2005 has seen developments in the way crisis events are reported at the BBC: The journalistic uses of social media have fostered a more collaborative form of journalism at the public broadcaster, with more personal accounts of news from afar (Allan, 2013; Andén-Papadopoulos and Pantti, 2013; Andersen, 2012; Beckett, 2008; Chouliaraki, 2010; Cottle, 2009; Hjorth and Kim, 2011).

NOTES

1. I presented this chapter at the World Social Science Forum Panel on Media and Democracy 1 in Montreal in October 2013.
2. Nevertheless, disaster communications involve "overlapping communication flows and interpenetrating communication forms and also often generate new communication hybrids that transverse both 'old' and 'new' media" (Pantti et al., 2012, 180). This renders difficult "the tendency to conceptualize the contemporary media and communications fields, and disaster communication within this, in essentially dualistic terms, or indeed informed by a notion of progressive suppression of 'old' media by 'new' media" (Pantti et al., 2012, 181). Given the complex and quickly changing media logic, I recognise the complexity of conceptualising a dualism of "new" and "old" media norms and practices.
3. Research has found that data journalism is easier to practice in countries where the data is accessible. For example, through open government journalists can gather data, but many governments are not transparent (Stray, 2013).
4. UGC Hub journalist, interview 2011.
5. Since September 2012.
6. Female foreign correspondent, interview 2011.

Conclusion
Global Crises, Local Responses

On Sunday, 11 March 2012, the BBC Burmese Service broadcasted its first programme from the new Broadcasting House on Portland Place and Langham Place in Central London. On 7 June 2013, Queen Elizabeth II officially opened the extension of the BBC new Broadcasting House. These events meant the closing down of the World Service newsrooms in Bush House and BBC Television Centre in White City, London, home of the BBC multimedia newsroom. For the first time since the BBC's founding on 18 October 1922, the BBC Academy, BBC News Channel, BBC Global News, BBC Arabic Television Service, BBC Persian Television Service, BBC Asian Network, Radio 1, Radio 1Xtra, Radio 3, Radio 4, BBC One, BBC Two, BBC Three, BBC Four, The One Show, and the BBC UGC Hub teams worked together under the same roof, in the same location. The newsroom is located at the heart of this new building, which is the largest 24/7 TV, radio, and online news coverage and live newsroom in Europe. The structural changes that the BBC has been taking part of in 7/7 reveal a transformation of the public broadcaster, and highlight how we need to contextualise changes in new information technologies within the political, cultural, social, and economic settings of public broadcasting in the United Kingdom and globally. To answer to what extent have social media transformed BBC journalistic practices and relations with audiences, requires an explanation of these changes in the media logic.

BBC journalists initially struggled to deal with social media in crisis reporting, and still do to a certain extent. Many journalists were skeptical about how to integrate social media into their reporting processes and outputs. Through a series of significant crisis news events, the BBC has reaffirmed its editorial standards and developed new features in its journalism. As a result of the high volume of social media material in crisis reporting and the BBC's desire to be closer to its audiences, the Corporation has found a need to develop new structures and processes to manage social media material and reporting. At the BBC, this new media logic required a centralised leadership.

As a result, new structures and roles have materialised in the newsroom, including the UGC Hub, BBC College of Journalism, Social Media Editor, and new editorial guidelines. Combined, these structures enable the public broadcaster to manage social media. Social media have contributed to the creation of a new media logic in which techies and ordinary citizens have gained significance in storytelling. The BBC perception of social media in BBC journalism is entrenched in the cultural and institutional understanding of BBC journalistic practices and norms, and the conflicts and tensions that social media create in journalism.

As journalists learn to use social media and report crises, there are opportunities to explore changes in the news organisation and relation with audiences. The case of the coverage of the conflict in Syria shows how the journalistic use of social media emphasised the relationship of the organisation with activists groups. For example, Jon Williams emphasised the importance of separating facts from fiction:

> Given the difficulties of reporting inside Syria, video filed by the opposition on Twitter, Facebook, and YouTube may provide some insight into the story on the ground. But stories are never black and white—often shades of grey. . . . A healthy scepticism is one of the essential qualities of any journalist—never more so than in reporting conflict.
>
> (Williams, 2012)

The news coverage of crisis events shows that social media have had an effect on the development of ethical and verification policies, as well as newsroom organisation and workflow practices. Research from Internews and the Centre for Global Communication Studies, written by Juliette Harkin, Kevin Anderson, Libby Morgan, and Briar Smith (2012), confirms that this is the case in the coverage of Syria. The authors wrote, "to more effectively use user-generated content and information from social media sources for Syria, BBC and Al Jazeera Arabic have both set up dedicated Syria Desks".

Several communication scholars consider citizen journalism as part of a media industry strategy to capitalise on free labour. In Lillie Chouliaraki's words, news organisations seek to "reinvent more attractive news models at low cost—yet running the risk of providing information that is ultimately less-than-trustworthy" (Chouliaraki, 2010b, 13). But there is an upshot to news organisations incorporating user-generated content in their news stories. This strategy enabled the BBC to symbolically become closer to its audiences and "re-structure the power relations in the newsroom, endowing corporate changes in online journalism with an irreducibly democratizing dimension" (Chouliaraki, 2010b, 13).

As tech-savvy journalists learned how to manage social media, they gained more influence within the newsroom. With the support of senior management and an institutional need to engage more with audiences, new structures emerged. Within these structures, tech-savvy journalists have played a central role in shaping social media within BBC traditional journalism. At the same time, as tech-savvy journalists acquired more knowledge of social media and as the need to manage social media content increased, they gained cultural and symbolic legitimacy in the newsroom. They have also been at the forefront of new media development at the BBC.

Within the arrangement of the new media logic in the BBC newsroom, social media have contributed to the architecture of the information that is presented to its audiences during crisis reporting. This has led to a more collaborative approach in crisis reporting and a more connected newsroom, insofar as new structures accommodating this new logic have replaced the media logic that predated social media. Collaboration between the BBC and its audiences in the UK and abroad can be measured with the emergence of technological platforms such as live feeds and social networking activities that have allowed the BBC to incorporate more user-generated content into its reporting. As the sociologist Manuel Castells writes, new power-making is taking place in the communication space. "Power holders have understood the need to enter the battle in horizontal communication networks" (Castells, 2007, 259). Technological developments, such as social networking activities and live feeds, within the context of BBC journalism, thus highlight a more collaborative type of crisis reporting.

In this connected newsroom, the boundaries between reporters and audiences are blurring. But journalism has a long history as a collaborative endeavour, from Abraham Zapruder's film of John F. Kennedy's assassination in Dallas in 1963 to the many amateur videos and photos taken of the 11 September 2011 attacks. Today, crisis news stories include "a greater variety of voices" and, hopefully, "different competing descriptions of events" (Karlsson, 2011, 286). In BBC crisis reporting, networks are converging as a result of "mass self-communication, over the Internet and wireless communication network . . . mass media and horizontal communication. The net outcome of this evolution is a historical shift of the public sphere from the institutional realm to the new communication space" (Castells, 2007, 238). The adoption of social media in BBC journalism reveals a more collaborative and self-reflexive BBC crisis reporting. In this kind of journalism, the BBC has retained its institutional, organisational, and cultural significance, and tech-savvy journalists and ordinary citizens have gained influence in creating a more connected newsroom in crisis reporting. The actions of the BBC are deliberate, but the future is unclear as to how people who are still unheard will achieve power in the new media logic.

Researching the BBC is important for our understanding of news production and news discourse. Studies such as this one also lay the groundwork for additional investigations on the continuities and discontinuities of journalism in a mass-mediated world. This type of analysis also enables us to reflect on how legacy and non-legacy news organisations adapt to emerging technologies, and the type of communication that social networks allows. The BBC is wise to rethink its journalism and engage in this new media logic. The public broadcaster would suffer from not engaging with this new form of storytelling and "people formerly known as the audience" (Rosen, 2006).

The work that lies ahead involves examining a greater range of social networking sites and modes of participation in various modes of crisis reporting. Doing so would allow us to rethink the characteristics of citizen journalism in the new media logic. Scholars should pay attention to modes of participation in reporting to generate further knowledge of the transformative media logic. The crisis reporting that the BBC has produced since the London bombing attacks of 7 July 2005 reveals the networked and fragmented world of professional journalism. Crisis reporting gives us a window into the possibilities for collaborative and more sensitive forms of reporting.

The challenge remaining for the BBC is to continue to create spaces for citizens to share stories. In doing so, ordinary citizens and media practitioners can undertake trust, responsibility, and empathy. This would prevent social exclusions transferable in the "us" and "them" split, which is prevalent in news reporting of crisis, pain, and suffering (Allan, 2012, 349; see also Bruns, 2008, 86). In a short time, social media have contributed to a rethinking of public broadcasting in global crisis reporting. Social media have enabled a representation of crisis reporting that is closer to audience experiences and, to a certain extent, less paternalistic that what John Reith had set up for the BBC.

Appendix
Unpacking Social Networking

What we now understand as "social media" have a history dating back to the expansion of the public Internet in the 1990s. As social media have grown and gained new significance, their definition has similarly expanded and evolved.

From the mid-1990s to today, websites have expanded ways for users to participate. I use the terminology social media to include these websites described below, although the term was coined later. Before the establishment of these social websites, dating websites, and ICQ (for "I seek you") enabled users to keep a list of friends, not visible to others, and communicate with them (boyd and Ellison, 2007), the first official social media platform was GeoCities. With GeoCities, users were able to create their own website based on six neighbourhoods, each with its own characteristics. Originally the neighbourhoods included Colosseum, Hollywood, RodeoDrive, SunsetStrip, WallStreet, and WestHollywood. In 1995, GeoCities allowed users to create free home pages (Homesteaders) within neighbourhoods. In 1995, another website, theglobe.com, enabled users to publish their own content and interact with other users with similar interests. In January 1999, Yahoo acquired theglobe.com. That same year, in South Korea, SK Communication, a subsidiary of SK Telecom, also launched Cyworld. The social networking platform was a public space where people from the same hometown or school could discuss and share information with each other.

From 1997 to 2001, the social network SixDegrees allowed users to create a personal profile and list friends, family, and acquaintances. danah m. boyd and Nicole B. Ellison (2007) wrote that at the time SixDegrees was the first website to combine these features:

> While SixDegrees attracted millions of users, it failed to become a sustainable business and, in 2000, the service closed. Looking back, its founder believes that SixDegrees was simply ahead of its time (A. Weinreich, personal communication, July 11, 2007). While people were already flocking to the Internet, most did not have extended networks of friends who were online. Early adopters complained that there was

little to do after accepting Friend requests, and most users were not interested in meeting strangers.

(boyd and Ellison, 2007).

SixDegrees was thus the first recognisable online social network. Today the website is open only to legacy members and new members invited by them.

At the end of the 1990s, blogging services started to flourish. On 27 August 1999, Blogger, a blog-publishing service developed by Pira Labs, launched its site. This website, owned by Google since 2003, allows users to create their own profile and to edit, moderate, and publish content in the forms of time-stamped comments, images, and weblog entries.

boyd and Ellison (2007) wrote that the second wave of social network systems emerged in the early 2000s. They trace the beginning of this wave to the 2001 launch of Ryze.com, a business networking website. The people behind Ryze, LinkedIn, Tribe.net, and Friendster were connected to each other, but the owners stated that they have never conceived their businesses as being in competition (boyd and Ellison, 2007). In 2002, Friendster connected real-world friends and virtual connections by way of an online platform. In 2003 MySpace followed Friendster.

In the mid-2000s, social networking sites expanded. In 2004, Harvard undergraduate Mark Zuckerberg and a handful of his college classmates introduced Facebook to connect Harvard undergraduates. Facebook was originally available only to students holding university e-mail addresses. Starting in 2005, the network broadened to high school students, professionals in corporate networks, and (eventually) anyone with an Internet connection. In July 2008, Facebook surpassed MySpace and Friendster in number of participants. In the years to follow, Facebook's growth accelerated. In July 2010, Facebook reached 500 million users and in October 2012, Facebook claimed one billion users (Smith et al., 2012).

In 2006, Biz Stone, Evan Williams, and Jack Dorsey launched Twitter. Twitter is a microblogging service that allows users to post and read messages up to 140 characters long (O'Dell, 2011). In 2012, Twitter delivered an average of 175 million tweets per day. In 2012, one million accounts were added to the platform every day (Stadd, 2012). In 2013, Twitter claimed 288 million active users and 485 million account holders (Stadd, 2013). "80 percent of the 10 million Twitter users in the United Kingdom now access the platform via their mobile device, and two-thirds (67 percent) of these mobile users follow brands on Twitter" (Bennett, 2013).

As these social networking sites and others evolve and expand, so does the definition of social media. Scholars have defined social media as a content production instrument of online communication. In one of the first academic definitions of social media, boyd and Ellison wrote that social media allow Internet users "to (1) construct a public or semi-public profile within a bounded system, (2) articulate a list of other users with whom they share a connection, and (3) view and traverse their list of connections and those made by others within the system. The nature and nomenclature of these connections may vary from site to site" (boyd and Ellison, 2007).

In an early account of the impact of social media on journalism, Nic Newman (2009) of the Reuters Institute for the Study of Journalism defined social media in three ways: content production, such as the activity of blogging; a communicative platform, represented, for instance, in the act of microblogging on Twitter or messaging a friend on Facebook; and a tool to achieve specific objectives, such as LinkedIn, to engage with a professional network, or Facebook, allowing journalists to access new and sometimes spatially distant sources of information. In the same vein, Daxton R. Stewart (2011, ix) discussed the challenge of systematically assessing the implications of social media. Newman also pointed out the difficulty of defining social media, because they are still young and evolving. Besides being communication instruments or tools for reporting, social media possess a network dimension and have the potential to shift the balance of power in news production from gatekeepers to online users.

Clay Shirky, in *Here Comes Everybody: The Power of Organizing Without Organizations* (2008), and Manuel Castells, in *Communication Power* (2009), suggest that Internet users appropriate social media to build an alternate communication model. In this new model, "everyone is its media outlet" (Shirky, 2008). Castells describes the phenomenon of "mass self-communication" in which there is a diversity and multiplication of entry points in the communication process and a conflict between global multimedia business networks and creative audiences. Global multimedia business networks try to re-commodify Internet-based, autonomous mass self-communication via pay sites, pay portals, and free streaming video portals. Creative audiences aim at establishing a level of control over the Internet and asserting their communicative freedom rights (Castells, 2009, 97). In Manuel Castells's mass self-communication framework, the interactive nature of new communication technologies enhances the autonomy of individuals (Castells, 2009, 129). This autonomy is "shaped, controlled, and curtailed by the growing concentration and interlocking of corporate media and network operators around the world" (Castells, 2009, 136). According to these communication scholars, social media have enabled new modes of producing news outside mainstream journalistic spaces, suggesting conflict between traditional media and social media (Poell and Borra, 2011).

Several scholars who explore the impact of social media on journalism have been less enthusiastic about the potential for social media to bring changes in journalism. Discussing the uses of user-generated content at the BBC, Claire Wardle and Andrew Williams (2010) write that social media content has been added as an extra layer of information in BBC News journalism. "The term 'UGC' developed as a way of describing content created and shared by users on the Internet, and in this context the term 'user' is appropriate, but in the context of the BBC, which produces television and radio content alongside online content, it is not" (Wardle and Williams,

2010, 782). Claire Wardle[1] states that trainers and senior managers "sold" social media to BBC journalists as just another news source. There is a tension in journalistic boundary maintenance in relation to social media.

Taking note of the research mentioned above, this book takes a holistic view of social media from the perspectives and subjectivities of BBC journalists. In this research, I included different social media: Facebook (a social networking site), Flickr (a photo-sharing site), Twitter (a microblogging site), YouTube (a video-sharing site), and Del.ic.ious (a social bookmarking site) (see also Social Media List). As communication scholar Alfred Hermida writes, "social media are an elusive term to define as it can refer to an activity, a software tool, or a platform, let alone the fact that all media have a social element" (Hermida, 2012, 310; see also Newman, 2009). An image captured by an ordinary citizen witnessing an event on his/her camera phone via Instagram can also be sent directly to the news organisation's e-mail, for example. Breaking news on Facebook can be picked up on Twitter or a reporter can discuss a story on the phone directly with citizens who happen to be witnesses or sources. Because social activities that are generated in and by social media are increasingly blurred, they could hardly be put in a single category such as audience material or social media inasmuch as these materials sit alongside and with professional journalists' eyewitnesses (Allan, 2012; Frosh and Pinchevski, 2009).

New media enables mass self-communication, meaning "self-generated in content, self-directed in emission, and self-selected in reception by the many that communicate with many" (Castells, 2007, 248). "New media technologies now enable vastly more users to experiment with a wider and seemingly more varied range of collaborative creative activities" (Harrison and Barthel, 2009, 174; Papacharissi and de Fatima Oliveira, 2012). Because citizen eyewitness accounts often sought and received on/from social media contribute to news production, it is important to study the social context in which networks interact and shape the media systems and communication networks (Cottle, 2011, 251).

NOTE

1. UGC Hub consultant, interview 2012.

Bibliography

Alexander, J. C. (2006) *The Civil Sphere*. Oxford: Oxford University Press.

Allan, S. (2013) *Citizen Witnessing: Revisioning Journalism in Times of Crisis*. Cambridge: Polity Press.

Allan, S. (2012) 'Online News Reporting of Crisis Events: Investigating the Role of Citizen Witnessing', pp. 331–352 in E. Siapera & A. Veglis (eds.), *The Handbook of Global Online Journalism*. Chichester, UK: Wiley.

Allan, S. (2007) 'Citizen Journalism and the Rise of "Mass Self-Communication": Reporting the London Bombings', *Global Media Journal—Australian Edition*, 1(1).

Allan, S., & Matheson, D. (2009) *Digital War Reporting*. Oxford: Polity.

Allan, S., & Matheson, D. (2004) 'Online Journalism in the Information Age', *Savoir, Travail & Société*, 2(3): 73–94.

Allan, S., Sonwalkar, P., & Carter, C. (2007) 'Bearing Witness: Citizen Journalism and Human Rights Issues', *Globalisation, Societies and Education*, 5(3): 373–389.

Allan, S., & Thorsen, E. (2010) 'Journalism, Public Service and BBC News Online', pp. 20–37 in G. Meilke & G. Redden (eds.), *News Online: Transformation and Continuity*. Basingstoke: Palgrave Macmillan.

Allan, S., & Zelizer, B. (2004) 'Rules of Engagement: Journalists and War', pp. 3–22 in S. Allan & B. Zelizer (eds.), *Reporting War: Journalists in Wartime*. London: Routledge.

Altheide, D. L. (1976) *Creating Reality: How Television News Distorts Events*. Los Angeles, CA: Sage.

Altheide, D. L., & Snow, R. P. (1979) *Media Logic*. London: Sage.

Andén-Papadopoulos, K., & Pantti, M. (2013) 'Re-Imagining Crisis Reporting: Professional Ideology of Journalists and Citizen Eyewitness Images', *Journalism*. DOI: 10.1177/1464884913479055.

Andersen, R. S. (2012) 'Remediating #Iranelection: Journalistic Strategies for Positioning Citizen-Made Snapshots and Text Bites from the 2009 Iranian Post-Election Conflict', *Journalism Practice*, 6(3): 317–336.

Annan, L. (1977) *Report of the Committee on the Future of Broadcasting*. London: HMSO.

Archetti, C. (2013) 'Journalism in the Age of Global Media: The Evolving Practices of Foreign Correspondents in London', *Journalism: Theory, Practice and Criticism*, 14(2): 419–436.

Ariel reporter. (2007) 'The News Agenda: Should the Audience Shape the Agenda?' Ariel, BBC, June 26.

Athar, S., & Myers, S. (2012) 'Tweeting Osama's Death: From Citizen to Journalist', URL (consulted 9 July 2012) http://schedule.sxsw.com/2012/events/event_IAP10307.

Ayton, P., & Tumber, H. (2001) 'The Rise and Fall of Perceived Bias at the BBC', *Intermedia*, 29(4): 12–15.

Bakhurst, K. (2011) 'How Social Media Changed the Way Newsrooms Work', URL (consulted 14 January 2012) www.bbc.co.uk/blogs/theeditors/2011/09/ibc_in_amsterdam.html.

Balaji, M. (2011) 'Racializing Pity: The Haiti Earthquake and the Plight of "Others"', *Critical Studies in Media Communication*, 28(1): 50–67.Barnett, S. (2011) *The Rise and Fall of Television Journalism: Just Wires and Lights in a Box?* London: Bloomsbury Press.

Barnett, S., & Curry, A. (1994) *The Battle for the BBC: A British Broadcasting Conspiracy?* London: Aurum Press Ltd.

Barrett, C. (2011) 'Open the Portal for a Wealth of Advice and Information', Ariel, BBC.

BBC. (2013) 'The Vernon Bartlett Affair 1933', URL (consulted 13 January 2013) www.bbc.co.uk/historyofthebbc/resources/bbcandgov/bartlett.shtml.

BBC. (2013b) 'The Story of BBC Television—The Contest', URL (consulted 13 January 2013) www.bbc.co.uk/historyofthebbc/resources/tvhistory/contest.shtml.

BBC. (2013c) 'Charter and Agreement', URL (consulted 14 January 2013) www.bbc.co.uk/bbctrust/governance/regulatory_framework/charter_agreement.html.

BBC. (2013d) 'News Group', URL (consulted 14 January 2013) www.bbc.co.uk/aboutthebbc/insidethebbc/managementstructure/bbcstructure/journalism.html.

BBC. (2013e) 'BBC Structure', URL (consulted 14 January 2013) www.bbc.co.uk/aboutthebbc/insidethebbc/managementstructure/bbcstructure/journalism.html.

BBC. (2012) 'Policies and Guidelines: Advertising', URL (consulted 11 September 2012) www.bbc.co.uk/aboutthebbc/insidethebbc/howwework/policiesandguidelines/advertising.html.

BBC. (2011) 'Editorial Guidelines', URL (consulted 14 January 2011) www.bbc.co.uk/editorialguidelines.

BBC. (2011b) 'Social Media Guidelines', URL (consulted 14 July 2011) http://news.bbc.co.uk/1/shared/bsp/hi/pdfs/14_07_11_news_social_media_guidance.pdf.

BBC. (2010) 'Taliban Kill Adulterous Afghan Couple', URL (consulted 19 January 2011) www.bbc.co.uk/news/world-south-asia-10983494.

BBC. (2010b) 'How Does Haiti Communicate After the Earthquake', URL (consulted 19 January 2011) http://news.bbc.co.uk/1/hi/technology/8470270.stm.

BBC. (2010c) 'Haiti Quake Witnesses Speak of Devastation', URL (consulted 1 June 2012) http://news.bbc.co.uk/1/hi/8455735.stm.

BBC. (2010d) 'TV Licence Fee: Facts & Figures', URL (consulted 14 January 2012) www.bbc.co.uk/pressoffice/keyfacts/stories/licencefee.shtml.

BBC. (2009) 'BBC News Appoints Alex Gubbay as First Social Media Editor', URL (consulted 14 January 2012) www.bbc.co.uk/pressoffice/pressreleases/stories/2009/11_november/16/gubbay.shtml.

BBC. (2009b) 'BBC Persia Television Combat Broadcast Interference from Iran', URL (consulted 14 January 2012) www.bbc.co.uk/pressoffice/pressreleases/stories/2009/06_june/19/persian.shtml.

BBC. (2008) 'Social Networking Guidelines', URL (consulted 14 July 2011) www.bbc.co.uk/editorialguidelines/page/guidance-blogs-bbc-full.

BBC. (2006) 'Creative Future—BBC Addresses Creative Challenges of On-Demand', URL (consulted 14 January 2012) www.bbc.co.uk/pressoffice/pressreleases/stories/2006/04_april/25/creative.shtml.

BBC. (2005) 'Tsunami: Readers' Eyewitness Accounts', URL (consulted 17 September 2012) http://news.bbc.co.uk/2/hi/talking_point/4146031.stm.

BBC. (2005b) 'Tsunami Loved Ones Reunited by Web', URL (consulted 17 September 2012) http://news.bbc.co.uk/2/hi/talking_point/4145643.stm.

BBC. (2004) 'Building Public Value', URL (consulted 1 September 2012) www.bbc.co.uk/pressoffice/pressreleases/stories/2004/06_june/29/bpv.shtml.

BBC. (2004b) 'Greg Dyke's E-mail to BBC Staff', URL (consulted 17 September 2012) http://news.bbc.co.uk/2/hi/uk_news/politics/3441845.stm.

BBC Trust. (2013) 'BBC Trust Review on the Impartiality and Accuracy of the BBC's Coverage of the Arab Spring', URL (consulted 4 June 2010) http://downloads.bbc.co.uk/bbctrust/assets/files/pdf/our_work/arabspring_impartiality/follow_up.pdf.

BBC Trust. (2012) 'A BBC Trust Report on the Impartiality and Accuracy of the BBC's Coverage of the Events Known as the "Arab Spring" ', URL (consulted 10 July 2012) http://downloads.bbc.co.uk/bbctrust/assets/files/pdf/our_work/arabspring_impartiality/arab_spring.pdf.

BBC Trust. (2007) 'From Seesaw to Wagon Wheel: Safeguarding Impartiality in the 21st Century', URL (consulted 4 June 2011) http://news.bbc.co.uk/1/shared/bsp/hi/pdfs/18_06_07impartialitybbc.pdf.

Beaumont, C. (2008) 'Mumbai Attacks: Twitter and Flickr Used to Break News', URL (consulted 4 June 2011) www.telegraph.co.uk/news/worldnews/asia/india/3530640/Mumbai-attacks-Twitter-and-Flickr-used-to-break-news-Bombay-India.html.

Becker, H. S. (1986) *Writing for Social Scientists*. Chicago: University of Chicago Press.

Beckett, C. (2011) 'The Line of Verification: A Guide to Social Media & Objectivity', URL (consulted 14 January 2012) http://blogs.lse.ac.uk/polis/2011/01/21/the-line-of-validation-a-guide-to-social-media-objectivity.

Beckett, C. (2008) *SuperMedia: Saving Journalism So it Can Save the World*. Oxford: Blackwell.

Belair-Gagnon, V. (2013) 'Revisiting Impartiality: Social Media and Journalism at the BBC', *Symbolic Interaction*, 36(4): 478–492.

Belair-Gagnon, V. (2012) 'Technology, Cultural Policy and the Public Service Broadcasting Tradition: Professional Practices at the BBC News in the Social Media Turn', pp. 112–131 in J. Paquette (ed.), *Cultural Policy, Work and Identity: The Creation, Renewal and Negotiation of Professional Subjectivities*. Farnham: Ashgate.

Belair-Gagnon, V., & Agur, C. (2013) 'When Print is Thriving, Where Does Social Media Fit? A Look at Practices at India's The Hindu', URL (consulted 14 January 2013) www.niemanlab.org/2013/01/when-print-is-thriving-where-does-social-media-fit-a-look-at-practices-at-indias-the-hindu.

Belair-Gagnon, V., & Anderson, C. W. (2014) 'Citizen Media and Journalism', in R. Mansell & P. Ang (eds.), *The International Encyclopedia of Digital Communication*. New York: Blackwell-Wiley and International Communication Association (ICA).

Belair-Gagnon, V., Mishra, S., & Agur, C. (2014) 'Reconstructing the Indian Public Sphere: Newswork and Social Media During the Delhi Gang Rape Case', *Journalism: Theory, Practice and Criticism*, 15(8):1059–1075.

Belair-Gagnon, V., Mishra, S., & Agur, C. (2013) 'Emerging Spaces of Storytelling: Journalistic Lessons from Social Media in the Delhi Gang Rape Case', URL (consulted 8 April 2013) www.niemanlab.org/2013/04/emerging-spaces-for-storytelling-journalistic-lessons-from-social-media-in-the-delhi-gang-rape-case.

Belanger, P. C. (2005) 'Online News at Canada's National Public Broadcaster: An Emerging Convergence', *Canadian Journal of Communication*, 30(3): 411–427.

Bell, M. (2011) 'Andy Carvin: The Middle East Revolutions One Tweet at a Time', URL (consulted 14 January 2013) http://voices.washingtonpost.com/blog-post/2011/03/andy_carvin_the_middle_east_re.html.

Benkler, Y. (2006) *The Wealth of Networks: How Social Production Transforms Markets and Freedom*. New Haven, CT: Yale University Press.

Bennett, D. (2013) 'How "You" Have Changed the BBC's Journalism', URL (consulted 21 October 2013) www.bbc.co.uk/blogs/blogcollegeofjournalism/posts/How-You-have-changed-the-BBCs-journalism.

Bennett, D. (2012) *Digital Media and Reporting Conflict: Blogging and the BBC's Coverage of War and Terrorism*. London: Routledge.

Bennett, D. (2011) *The Impact of Blogging on the BBC's Coverage of War and Terrorism*. PhD Thesis. London: King's College.

Bennett, S. (2013) '80% of UK Twitter Users Connect via a Mobile Device', URL (consulted 22 March 2013) www.mediabistro.com/alltwitter/twitter-uk-mobile_b36412.

Birt, J. (2002) *The Harder Path*. London: Time Warner Books.

Boaden, H. (2008) 'The Role of Citizen Journalism in Modern Democracy', URL (consulted 14 January 2012) www.bbc.co.uk/blogs/theeditors/2008/11/the_role_of_citizen_journalism.html.

Boaden, H. (2006) 'Welcome', URL (consulted 14 January 2012) www.bbc.co.uk/blogs/theeditors/2006/06/welcome.html.

Born, G. (2005) *Uncertain Vision: Birt, Dyke and the Reinvention of the BBC*. London: Vintage.

boyd, d. m., & Ellison, N. B. (2007) 'Social Network Sites: Definition, History, and Scholarship', *Journal of Computer-Mediated Communication*, 13(1).

Bradshaw, P. (2010) 'How to be a Data Journalist', URL (consulted 14 January 2012) www.guardian.co.uk/news/datablog/2010/oct/01/data-journalism-how-to-guide.

Breed, W. (1955) 'Social Control in the Newsroom: A Functional Analysis', *Social Forces*, 33(4): 326–335.

Brewer, J. D. (2000) *Ethnography*. Buckingham: Open University Press.

Briggs, A. (1995) *The History of Broadcasting in the United Kingdom: Competition*, vol. 5. Oxford: Oxford University Press.

Briggs, A. (1995b) *The History of Broadcasting in the United Kingdom: The Golden Age of the Wireless*, vol. 2. Oxford: Oxford University Press.

Briggs, A. (1986) *The BBC: The First Fifty Years*. Oxford: Oxford University Press.

Briggs, A. (1961) *The History of Broadcasting in the United Kingdom: The Birth of Broadcasting*, vol. 1. Oxford: Oxford University Press.

Bruno, N. (2011) *Tweet First, Verify Later? How Real-Time Information is Changing the Coverage of Worldwide Crisis Events*. Oxford: Reuters Institute for the Study of Journalism, University of Oxford.

Bruns, A. (2008) *Blogs, Wikipedia, Second Life, and Beyond: From Production to Produsage*. New York: Peter Lang.

Bunz, M. (2010) 'BBC Tells News Staff to Embrace Social Media', URL (consulted 14 January 2012) www.guardian.co.uk/media/pda/2010/feb/10/bbc-news-social-media.

Burn, T. (1977) *The BBC: Public Institution and Private World*. London: The MacMillan Press Ltd.

Bursari, S. (2008) 'Tweeting the Terror: How Social Media Reacted to Mumbai', URL (consulted 4 June 2011) http://edition.cnn.com/2008/WORLD/asiapcf/11/27/mumbai.twitter/.

Castells, M. (2009) *Communication Power*. Oxford: Oxford University Press.

Castells, M. (2007) 'Communication, Power and Counter-Power in the Network Society', *International Journal of Communication*, 1(1): 238–266.

Caulfield, B., & Karmali, N. (2008) 'Mumbai: Twitter's Moment. Forbes', URL (consulted 14 January 2013) www.forbes.com/2008/11/28/mumbai-twitter-sms-tech-internet-cx_bc_kn_1128mumbai.html.

Cellan-Jones, R. (2011) 'Twitter Captures the Osama Bin Laden Raid', URL (consulted 30 May 2012) www.bbc.co.uk/blogs/thereporters/rorycellanjones/2011/05/tweeting_the_osama_raid.html.

Cellan-Jones, R. (2008) 'Twitter—The Mumbai Myths', URL (consulted 30 May 2012) www.bbc.co.uk/blogs/technology/2008/12/twitter_the_mumbai_myths.html.

Chalaby, J. K. (1998) *The Invention of Journalism*. London: MacMillan.

Chouliaraki, L. (2010) 'Journalism and the Visual Politics of War and Conflict', pp. 520–532 in S. Allan (ed.), *The Routledge Companion to News and Journalism*. London: Routledge.

Chouliaraki, L. (2010b) 'Ordinary Witnessing in Post-Television News: Toward a New Moral Imagination', *Critical Discourse Studies*, 7(3): 305–319.

Chowdhury, M. (2008) 'The Role of the Internet in Burma's Saffron Revolution', pp. 1–17 in Berkman Center (ed.), *Internet & Democracy Case Study Series*. Cambridge: Berkman Center.

Cooper, G. (2011) *From Their Own Correspondent*. Oxford: Reuters Institute for the Study of Journalism, University of Oxford.

Cornu, D. (2013) *Tous Connectés! Internet et les Nouvelles Frontières de l'Info*. Genève: Labor et Fides.

Cottle, S. (2011) 'Media and the Arab Uprisings of 2011: Research Notes', *Journalism*, 12(5): 647–659.

Cottle, S. (2010) 'Global Crises and World News Ecology', pp. 473–484 in S. Allan (ed.), *The Routledge Companion to News and Journalism*. London: Routledge.

Cottle, S. (2009) 'Global Crises in the News: Staging News Wars, Disasters and Climate Change', *International Journal of Communication*, 3: 494–516.

Cottle, S., & Ashton, M. (1999) 'From BBC Newsroom to BBC Newscentre: On Changing Technology and Journalist Practices', *Convergence: The International Journal of Research into New Media Technologies*, 5(3): 22–43.

Crisell, A. (1997) *An Introductory History of British Broadcasting*. London: Routledge.

Curran, J., & Seaton, J. (2003) *Power Without Responsibility: The Press, Broadcasting, and New Media in Britain*. London: Routledge.

Dahlgren, P. (1996) 'Media Logic in Cyberspace: Repositioning Journalism and its Publics', *Javnost/The Public*, 3(3): 59–72.

Defago, N. (2012) 'Think Before You Tweet', URL (consulted 20 November 2012) www.bbc.co.uk/ariel/20166166.

Department of Culture, Media and Sports. (2006) *A Public Service for All: The BBC in the Digital Age (White Paper)*. Norwich: Her Majesty's Stationery Office.

Department of Culture, Media and Sports. (2006b) *Broadcasting: Copy of Royal Charter for the Continuance of the British Broadcasting Corporation (Royal Charter)*. Norwich: Her Majesty's Stationery Office.

Deuze, M. (2008) 'Understanding Journalism as Newswork: How it Changes, and How it Remains the Same', *Westminster Papers in Communication and Culture*, 5(2): 4–23.

Deuze, M. (1999) 'Journalism and the Web: An Analysis of Skills and Standards in an Online Environment', *International Communication Gazette*, 61(5): 373–390.

Di Lauro, M. (2012) 'BBC Mistakenly Runs Dated Iraq Photo to Illustrate the Syrian Massacre', URL (consulted 14 January 2013) www.marcodilauro.com/blog/bbc-mistakenly-runs-dated-iraq-photo-to-illustrate-the-syrian-massacre.

Doucet, L. (2011) 'Big Stories: The Arab Spring', URL (consulted 10 April 2012) www.bbc.co.uk/journalism/blog/2011/11/big-stories-the-arab-spring.shtml.

Douglas, T. (2006) 'How 7/7 "Democratised" the Media', URL (consulted 18 June 2012) http://news.bbc.co.uk/2/hi/uk_news/5142702.stm.

Douglas, T. (2005) 'Shaping the Media with Mobiles', URL (consulted 14 January 2013) http://news.bbc.co.uk/2/hi/uk_news/4745767.stm.

Douglas, T. (2004) 'What Does the Neil Report Mean?', URL (consulted 18 June 2012) http://news.bbc.co.uk/1/hi/entertainment/3833771.stm.

Doyle, G. (2010) 'From Television to Multi-Platform: Less From More or More for Less', *Convergence: The International Journal of Research into New Media Technologies*, 16(4): 1–19.

Dyke, G. (2004) *Greg Dyke: Inside Story*. London: Harper Collins.

Eltringham, M. (2011) 'Social Media: What's the Difference Between Curation and Journalism?', URL (consulted 13 April 2012) www.bbc.co.uk/journalism/blog/2011/03/social-media-whats-the-differe.shtml.

Eltringham, M. (2011b) 'Matthew Eltringham on How BBC Uses and Regulates UGC and Social Media', URL (consulted 13 April 2012) www.youtube.com/watch?v=4aaZCn43M2s.

Eltringham, M. (2011c) '"The Line of Verification": A New Approach to Objectivity for Social Media', URL (consulted 13 April 2012) www.bbc.co.uk/blogs/blogcollegeofjournalism/posts/The-line-of-verification-a-new-approach-to-objectivity-for-social-media.

Eltringham, M. (2011d) '#bbcsms: Chatham House Rule', URL (consulted 1 October 2012) www.bbc.co.uk/blogs/blogcollegeofjournalism/posts/bbcsms_chatham_house_rule.

Eltringham, M. (2010) 'UGC Five Years On', URL (consulted 13 April 2012) www.bbc.co.uk/journalism/blog/2010/07/ugc-five-years-on.shtml.

Eltringham, M. (2009) 'Audience and the News', pp. 50–55 in C. Miller (ed.), *The Future of Journalism*. London: BBC College of Journalism.

Eltringham, M. (2009b) 'Reaching Out', URL (consulted 1 October 2012) www.bbc.co.uk/blogs/theeditors/matthew_eltringham.

Epstein, E. J. (1973) *News from Nowhere: Television and the News*. New York: Random House.

Ericson, R. V., Baranek, P. M., & Chan, J.B.L. (1989) *Negotiating Control: A Study of News Sources*. Toronto: University of Toronto Press.

Fenton, N. (2010) 'News in a Digital Age', pp. 557–565 in S. Allan (ed.), *The Routledge Companion to News and Journalism*. London: Routledge.

Fenton, N. (ed.) (2009) *New Media, Old News: Journalism and Democracy in the Digital Age*. London: Sage.

Fisher, M. (2012) 'A False Photo from a Real Massacre', URL (consulted 16 May 2013) www.theatlantic.com/international/archive/2012/05/a-false-photo-from-a-real-massacre/257733/.

Fishman, M. (1980) *Manufacturing the News*. Austin: University of Texas Press.

Flock, E. (2012) 'Iranians Using Proxy Servers 10 Times More Than They were Last Year', URL (consulted 14 January 2013) www.washingtonpost.com/blogs/blogpost/post/iranians-using-proxy-servers-10-times-more-than-they-were-last-year/2012/02/15/gIQA4LFMGR_blog.html.

Franks, S. (2010) 'Globalising Consciousness: The End of "Foreign" Reporting and No More Foreign Secrets', *Ethical Space: The International Journal of Communication Ethics*, 7(4): 39–47.

Freedman, D. (2008) *The Politics of Media Policy*. Oxford: Polity Press.

Frosh, P., & Pinchevski, A. (2009) 'Introduction: Why Media Witnessing? Why Now?', pp. 1–19 in P. Frosh & A. Pinchevski (eds.), *Media Witnessing: Testimony in the Age of Mass Communication*. Houndmills, UK: Palgrave Macmillan.

Furness, H. (2012) 'BBC News Uses "Iraq Photo to Illustrate Syrian Massacre"', URL (consulted 14 January 2013) www.telegraph.co.uk/culture/tvandradio/bbc/9293620/BBC-News-uses-Iraq-photo-to-illustrate-Syrian-massacre.html.

Galtung, J., & Ruge, M. H. (1965) 'The Structure of Foreign News: The Presentation of the Congo, Cuba and Cyprus Crises in Four Norwegian Newspapers', *Journal of Peace Research*, 2(1): 64–91.

Gans, H. J. (2011) 'Multiperspectival News Revisited: Journalism and Representative Democracy', *Journalism*, 12(1): 3–13.

Gans, H. J. (1979) *Deciding What's News: A Study of CBS Evening News, NBC Nightly News, Newsweek and Time*. Evenston, IL: Northwestern University Press.

Gant, S. (2007) *We're All Journalists Now: The Transformation of the Press and Reshaping of the Law in the Internet Age*. New York: Free Press.

Ghanavizi, N. (2011) 'Political Protest and the Persian Blogosphere', pp. 255–287 in S. Cottle & L. Lester (eds.), *Transnational Protests and the Media*. New York: Peter Lang.

Giddens, A. (1984) *The Constitution of Society: Outline of the Theory of Structuration*. Berkley, CA: University of California Press.

Gilmor, D. (2005) 'Tsunami and Citizen Journalism's First Draft', URL (consulted 13 April 2012) http://dangillmor.typepad.com/dan_gillmor_on_grassroots/2005/01/tsunami_and_cit.html.

Gilmor, D. (2004) *We the Media: Grassroots Journalism By the People, For the People*. Sebastopol, CA.: O'Reiley Media.

Glazer, M. (2010) 'Citizen Journalism: Widening World Views, Extending Democracy', pp. 578–590 in S. Allan (ed.), *The Routledge Companion to News and Journalism*. New York: Routledge.

Golding, P., & Elliott, P. (1979) *Making the News*. New York: Longman.

Gowing, N. (2008) *'Skyful of Lies' and Black Swans: The News Tyranny of Shifting Information Power in Crisis*. Oxford: Reuters Institute.

Grade, M. (2005) 'Goodman Media Lecture: The Future of Impartiality', URL (consulted 19 June 2012) www.bbc.co.uk/pressoffice/speeches/stories/grade_goodman.shtml.

Grossman, L. (2009) 'Iran Protests: Twitter, the Medium of the Movement', URL (consulted 19 June 2012) www.time.com/time/world/article/0,8599,1905125,00.html#ixzz2LF7rqAWQ.

Gubbay, A. (2011) 'Comments and Making Our Coverage More Social', URL (consulted 13 April 2012) www.bbc.co.uk/blogs/theeditors/alex_gubbay.

Halliday, J. (2012) 'Sky News Clamps Down on Twitter Use: Reporters Banned from Reposting Non-Company Tweets and Told to Check with the News Desk Before Breaking News Stories', URL (consulted 17 March 2012) www.guardian.co.uk/media/2012/feb/07/sky-news-twitter-clampdown.

Halliday, J. (2011) 'SXSW 2011: How the BBC Gets Round Censorship Using Social Media: BBC World Service Staff Reveal How YouTube and Microblogging Sites Help Web Users in Iran and China Get News', URL (consulted 30 May 2012) www.guardian.co.uk/technology/pda/2011/mar/13/sxsw-bbc-iran-china.

Hamilton, C. (2012) 'Houla Massacre Picture Miskate', URL (consulted 29 May 2012) www.bbc.co.uk/blogs/theeditors/2012/05/houla_massacre_picture_mistake.html.

Hamilton, C. (2012b) 'Breaking New Guidance for BBC Journalists', URL (consulted 13 April 2012) www.bbc.co.uk/blogs/theeditors/2012/02/twitter_guidelines_for_bbc_jou.html.

Hamilton, C. (2011) 'Updated Social Media Guidances', URL (consulted 13 April 2012) www.bbc.co.uk/blogs/theeditors/2011/07/bbc_social_media_guidance.html.

Hamilton, C. (2011b) 'Use of Photographs from Social Media in our Output', URL (consulted 1 June 2012) www.bbc.co.uk/blogs/theeditors/2011/08/use_of_photographs_from_social.html.

Hampton, M. (2008) 'The "Objectivity" Ideal and its Limitations in the 20th Century British Journalism', *Journalism Studies*, 9(7): 477–493.

Harkin, J., Anderson, K., Morgan, L., & Smith, B. (2012) *Deciphering User-Generated Content in Transitional Societies: A Syria Coverage Case Study*. Philadelphia, PA: Internews Center for Innovation & Learning, Center for Global Communication Studies, Annenberg School for Communication, University of Pennsylvania.

Harrison, J. (2010) 'Gatekeeping and News Selection as Symbolic Mediation', pp. 191–201 in S. Allan (ed.), *The Routledge Companion to News and Journalism*. New York: Routledge.

Harrison, J. (2009) 'User-Generated Content and Gatekeeping at the BBC Hub', *Journalism Studies*, 11(2): 243–256.

Harrison, T. M., & Barthel, B. (2009) 'Wielding New Media in Web 2.0: Exploring the History of Engagement with the Collaborative Construction of Media Products', *New Media & Society*, 11(1–2): 155–178.

Hassanpour, N., Borra, E., Barbera, P., Jost, J., & Tucker, J. (forthcoming 2014) 'Online Political Dialogue Under Competitive Authoritarianism: 2013 Iranian Presidential Elections,' URL: https://www.princeton.edu/politics/about/file-repository/public/IR_Colloquium_NHassanpour.pdf.

Hermida, A. (2012) 'Social Journalism: Exploring How Social Media are Shaping Journalism', pp. 309–328 in E. Siapera & A. Veglis (eds.), *The Handbook of Global Online Journalism*. Chischester, UK: Wiley.

Hermida, A. (2010) 'Twittering the News', *Journalism Practice*, 4(3): 297–308.

Hermida, A. (2009) 'The Blogging BBC: Journalism Blogs at "the World's Most Trusted News Organisation"', *Journalism Practice*, 3(3): 268–284.

Hermida, A., & Thurman, N. (2008) 'A Clash of Cultures: The Integration of User-Generated Content Within Professional Journalistic Frameworks at British Newspaper Websites', *Journalism Practice*, 2(3): 343–356.

Herrmann, S. (2012) 'User Generated Content and "Arab Spring" Coverage', URL (consulted 10 July 2012) www.bbc.co.uk/blogs/theeditors/2012/06/user_generated_content_and_ara.html.

Herrmann, S. (2009) 'Social Media in Iran', URL (consulted 13 April 2012) www.bbc.co.uk/blogs/theeditors/2009/06/social_media_in_iran.html.

Herrmann, S. (2008) 'Newsroom Changes', URL (consulted 13 April 2012) www.bbc.co.uk/blogs/theeditors/2008/06/newsroom_changes.html.

Herrmann, S. (2008b) 'Mumbai, Twitter and Live Updates', URL (consulted 13 April 2012) www.bbc.co.uk/blogs/theeditors/2008/12/theres_been_discussion_see_eg.html.

Herrmann, S. (2007) 'Information from Burma', URL (consulted 13 April 2012) www.bbc.co.uk/blogs/theeditors/2007/09/information_from_burma.html.

Hjorth, L., & Kim, K. Y. (2011) 'The Mourning After: A Case Study of Social Media in the 3.11 Earthquake Disaster in Japan', *Television & New Media*, 12(6): 552–559.

Holmes, S. (2007) 'Burma's Cyber-Dissidents', URL (consulted 24 April 2011) http://news.bbc.co.uk/1/hi/world/asia-pacific/7012984.stm.

Holmwood, L., & Dehghan, S. K. (2009) 'Iran Widens Jamming of BBC as Revolutionary Guard Cautions Bloggers', URL (consulted 13 April 2012) www.guardian.co.uk/media/2009/jun/17/iran-bbc-jamming-bloggers-revolutionary-guard?INTCMP=SRCH.

Horrocks, P. (2010) 'Stop the Blocking Now', URL (consulted 29 May 2012) www.bbc.co.uk/blogs/theeditors/2009/06/stop_the_blocking_now.html.

Horrocks, P. (2009) 'The End of Fortress Journalism', pp. 6–17 in C. Miller (ed.), *The Future of Journalism*. London: BBC College of Journalism.

Horrocks, P. (2008) 'The Value of Citizen Journalism', URL (consulted 29 May 2012) www.bbc.co.uk/blogs/legacy/theeditors/2008/01/value_of_citizen_journalism.html.

Horrocks, P. (2007) 'Trusting the BBC', URL (consulted 29 May 2012) www.bbc.co.uk/blogs/theeditors/2007/02/trusting_the_bbc.html.

Hoskins, A., & O'Loughlin, B. (2010) *War and Media: The Emergence of Diffuse War*. Cambridge: Polity Press.

House of Lords. (2012a) Great Britain Parliament. Defamation Bill. London: Stationery Office (Bill: Great Britain. Parliament. House of Lords, 75).

House of Lords. (2012b) Great Britain Parliament. Defamation Bill. London: Stationery Office (Bill: Great Britain. Parliament. House of Lords, 139).

Howe, J. (2006) 'The Rise of Crowdsourcing', URL (consulted 24 April 2011) www.wired.com/wired/archive/14.06/crowds.html.

Hughes, S. (2012) 'Social Media Newsgathering', URL (consulted 24 April 2011) www.youtube.com/watch?v=1sPeTaJ2aWs&list=UUov0iLt-7jx5KCuWaavCbtw&index=1&feature=plcp.

Hughes, S. (2012b) 'The Class of '92 Returns to Sarajevo', URL (consulted 24 April 2011) www.bbc.co.uk/journalism/blog/2012/04/the-class-of-92-returns-to-sar.shtml.

Hughes, S. (2011) 'BBC Producer Stuart Hughes Discusses Social Media Newsgathering', URL (consulted 24 April 2011) www.youtube.com/watch?v=sY1IxbE1xNM.

Hugues, T. (1994) 'Technological Momentum', pp. 101–114 in M. Roe Smith & L. Marx (eds.), *Does Technology Drive History? The Dilemma of Technological Determinism*. Cambridge, MIT Press.

Hutton, L. (2004) 'Report of the Inquiry into the Circumstances Surrounding the Death of Dr David Kelly C.M.G.', URL (consulted 20 April 2012) http://webarchive.nationalarchives.gov.uk/20090128221550/www.the-hutton-inquiry.org.uk/content/report/index.htm.

Indian Government. (2008) 'Mumbai Terror Attack Final Form / Report', URL (consulted 6 July 2012) www.hindu.com/nic/mumbai-terror-attack-final-form.pdf.

Jarvis, J. (2008) 'In Mumbai, Witnesses are Writing the News', URL (consulted 14 January 2013) www.guardian.co.uk/media/2008/dec/01/mumbai-terror-digital-media.

Jones, J., & Salter, L. (2012) *Digital Journalism*. London: Sage Publications.

Jordan, D. (2008) 'BBC Guidance On Social Networking', URL (consulted 1 October 2012) www.bbc.co.uk/blogs/bbcinternet/2008/03/bbc_guidance_on_social_network.html.

Karlsson, M. (2011) 'The Immediacy of Online News, the Visibility of Journalistic Processes and a Restructuring of Journalistic Authority', *Journalism*, 12(3): 279–295.

Kaufman, G. (2004) *A Public BBC: First Report of Session 2004–05: Vol. 1: Report, Together with Formal Minutes*. London: House of Commons, The Stationary Office Limited.

Klinenberg, E. (2005) 'Convergence: News Production in a Digital Age', *Annals of the American Academy of Political and Social Science*, 597(1): 48–64.

Klontzas, M. (2008) 'iVision and the BBC: Building Public Value', *Observatorio (OBS*) Journal*, 5(1): 41–55.

Knight, M. (2012) 'Journalism as Usual: The Use of Social Media as Newsgathering Tool in the Coverage of the Iranian Elections in 2009', *Journal of Media Practice*, 13(1): 61–78.

Kovach, B., & Rosenstiel, T. (2001) *The Elements of Journalism: What Newspeople Should Know and the Public Should Expect*. New York: Three Rivers Press.

Kperogi, B. (2007) 'On "Having Been There": "Eyewitnessing" as a Journalistic Key Word', *Critical Studies in Media Communication*, 24(5): 408–428.

Kperogi, F. A. (2011) 'Cooperation with the Corporation? CNN and the Hegemonic Cooptation of Citizen Journalism Through iReport.com', *New Media & Society*, 13(2): 314–329.

Küng-Shankleman, L. (2000) *Inside the BBC and CNN: Managing Media Organisations*. New York: Routledge.

Kyaw, H. A. (2009) 'Media Restricted in Pre-Election Coverage', URL (consulted 16 August 2012) www.dvb.no/news/media-restricted-in-pre-election-coverage/2518.

134 Bibliography

Lariscy, R. W. et al. (2009) 'An Examination of the Role of Online Social Media in Journalists' Source Mix', *Public Relation Review*, 35: 314–316.

Lasorsa, D. L., Lewis, S. C., & Holton, A. (2012) 'Normalising Twitter: Journalism Practice in an Emerging Communication Space', *Journalism Studies*, 13(1): 19–36.

Lee, M. (2008) 'Blogs Feed Information Frenzy on Mumbai Blasts', URL (consulted 14 January 2013) http://in.reuters.com/article/2008/11/27/idINIndia-367 33420081127.

Leggio, S. (2008) 'Mumbai Attack Coverage Demonstrates (Good and Bad) Maturation Point of Social Media', URL (consulted 14 January 2013) www.zdnet.com/blog/feeds/mumbai-attack-coverage-demonstrates-good-and-bad-maturation-point-of-social-media/339.

Lewis, S. C. (2012) 'The Tension Between Professional Control and Open Participation: Journalists and its Boundaries', *Information, Communication & Society*, 15(6): 836–866.

Lofland, J., & Lofland, L. H. (1995) *Analyzing Social Settings: A Guide to Qualitative Observation and Analysis*. Belmont, CA: Wadsworth.

Lotan, G. et al. (2011) 'The Revolutions were Tweeted: Information Flows During the 2011 Tunisian and Egyptian Revolutions', *International Journal of Communication*, 5: 1375–1405.

Luft, O. (2008) 'Social Media Journalist: "You have to be selective, keeping across all sites dilutes the value of the good ones" Vicky Taylor, editor BBC Interactivity', URL (consulted 13 April 2012) http://blogs.journalism.co.uk/2008/02/29/social-media-journalist-"-vicky-taylor-editor-bbc-interactivity.

MacLeod, L. (2010) 'New Media Vital in Breaking Haiti Earthquake Story', URL (consulted 30 May 2012) www.bbc.co.uk/worldservice/worldagenda/2010/01/100 122_worldagenda_haiti_monitoring.shtml.

Marsh, K. (2010) 'New Politics #3', URL (consulted June 2012) www.bbc.co.uk/blogs/blogcollegeofjournalism/posts/new_politics_3.

Marshall, S. (2013) 'BBC College Announces New York Social Media Summit', URL (consulted 15 March 2013) www.journalism.co.uk/news/bbc-college-of-journalism-announces-new-york-social-media-summit/s2/a552405/.

Matheson, D. (2004) 'Weblogs and the Epistemology of the News: Some Trends in Online Journalism', *New Media & Society*, 6(4): 443–468.

McAthy, R. (2010) 'Looking Back on the 7/7 Bombings and the Birth of User-Generated Content', URL (consulted 30 May 2012) http://blogs.journalism.co.uk/2010/07/07/looking-back-on-the-77-bombings-and-the-birth-of-user-generated-content.

Meier, K. (2007) 'Innovations in Central European Newsrooms: Overview and Case Study', *Journalism Practice*, 1(1): 4–19.

Mitchelstein, E., & Boczkowski, P. J. (2009) 'Between Tradition and Change: A Review of Recent Research on Online News Production', *Journalism*, 10(5): 562–586.

Moe, K. Z. (2007) 'Suu Kyi Greets Monks at her Home; 10,000 Monks Demonstrate in Mandalay', URL (consulted June 2013) www.burmanet.org/news/2007/09/22/irrawaddy-suu-kyi-greets-monks-at-her-home-10000-monks-demonstrate-in-mandalay-kywa-zwa-moe/#more-8971.

Molotch. H., & Lester, M. (1974) 'News as Purposive Behavior: On the Strategic Use of Routine Events, Accident, and Scandals', *American Sociological Review*, 39(1): 101–112.

Morgan, J. (2010) 'Haiti—the Tweet that Raised $8m', URL (consulted 17 December 2011) http://news.bbc.co.uk/1/hi/world/americas/8460791.stm.

Morrison, D. E., & Tumber, H. (1988) *Journalists at War: The Dynamics of News Reporting During the Falkands Conflict*. Newbury Park, CA: Sage Publications.

Mortensen, M. (2011) 'When Citizen Photojournalism Sets the News Agenda: Neda Agha Soltan as a Web 2.0 Icon of Postelection Unrest in Iran', *Global Media and Communication*, 7(1): 4–16.

Mottaz, L. (2010) 'New Media in Closed Societies: The Role of Digital Technologies in Burma's Saffron Revolution', *Democracy & Society*, 7(2). URL: http://www.democracyandsociety.com/blog/wp-content/uploads/2010/07/MottazSaffronRevolution7.22.pdf

Murray, A. (2011) 'BBC Processes for Verifying Social Media', URL (consulted 18 May 2011) www.bbc.co.uk/blogs/.../bbcsms_bbc_procedures_for_veri.

Murthy, D. (2011) 'Twitter: Microphone for the Masses?' *Media, Culture & Society*, 33(5): 779–789.

Muthukumaraswamy, K. (2010) 'When the Media Meet Crowds of Wisdom: How Journalists are Tapping into Audience Expertise and Manpower for the Processes of Newsgathering', *Journalism Practice*, 4(1): 48–65.Neelamalar, M., Chitra, P., & Darwin, A. (2009) 'The Print Media Coverage of the 27/11 Mumbai Terror Attacks: A Study on the Coverage of Leading Indian Newspapers and its Impact on People', *Journal of Media and Communication Studies*, 1(6): 95–105.

Neil, R. et al. (2004) 'The Neil Report: The BBC's Journalism after Hutton', URL (consulted 15 May 2011) http://downloads.bbc.co.uk/aboutthebbc/insidethebbc/howwework/reports/pdf/neil_report.html.

Newman, N. (ed.). (2012) *Reuters Institute Digital News Report 2012: Tracking the Future of News*. Oxford: Reuters Institute.

Newman, N. (2011) *Mainstream Media and the Distribution of News in the Age of Social Discovery*. Oxford: Oxford University, Reuters Institute for the Study of Journalism.

Newman, N. (2009) *The Rise of Social Media and its Impact on Mainstream Journalism: A Study on How Newspapers and Broadcasters in the UK and US are Responding to a Wave of Participatory Social Media and a Historic Shift in Control Towards Individual Consumers*. Oxford: Oxford University, Reuters Institute for the Study of Journalism.

O'Dell, J. (2011) 'The History of Social Media', URL (consulted 17 December 2011) http://mashable.com/2011/01/24/the-history-of-social-media-infographic.

Oliver, L. (2009) 'UGC Offering Authenticity Despite Restrictions in Iran, Says BBC's Richard Sambrook', URL (consulted 13 April 2012) www.journalism.co.uk/news/ugc-offering-authenticity-despite-restrictions-in-iran-says-bbc-s-richard-sambrook/s2/a534793.

Oliver, L. (2008) 'Broadsheet vs Broadband: BBC's Pete Clifton on Citizen Journalism', URL (consulted 13 April 2012) http://blogs.journalism.co.uk/2008/10/31/broadsheet-vs-broadband-bbcs-pete-clifton-on-citizen-journalism/.

Olsson, E. K. (2010) 'Defining Crisis News Events', Nordicom Review, 31(1): 87–101.

Palmer, J. (2010) 'Social Networks and the Web Offer a Lifeline in Haiti', URL (consulted 19 January 2011) http://news.bbc.co.uk/1/hi/8461240.stm.

Pantti, M., Wahl-Jorgensen, K., & Cottle, S. (2012) *Disasters and the Media*. New York: Peter Lang.

Papacharissi, Z., & de Fatima, O. (2012) 'Affective News and Networked Publics: The Rhythms of News Storytelling on #Egypt', *Journal of Communication*, 62: 266–282.

Peacock Committee on the Funding of the BBC. (1986) *Report of the Committee on Broadcasting*. London: Her Majesty's Stationery Office.

Petley, J. (2010) 'Impartiality in Television News: Profitability Versus Public Service', pp. 602–613 in S. Allan (ed.), *The Routledge Companion to News and Journalism*. New York: Routledge.

Petulla, S. (2013) 'In Burma, Newspapers are Going Daily, but the Transformation to Watch May be Mobile', URL (consulted 23 March 2013) www.niemanlab.

org/2013/03/in-burma-newspapers-are-going-daily-but-the-transformation-to-watch-may-be-in-mobile/livepage.apple.com.

Philips, A. (2012) 'More Journalists Should Harness Social Media, BBC Journalist Says', URL (consulted 22 August 2012) www.exposureradio.org/2012/02/01/more-journalists-should-harness-social-media-bbc-journalist-says.

Philips, A. (2010) 'Old Sources: New Bottles' pp. 87–101 in N. Fenton (ed.), *New Media, Old News: Journalism & Democracy in the Digital Age*. London: Sage Publications.

Pidduck, J. (2012) 'Exile Media, Global News Flows and Democratization: The Role of Democratic Voice of Burma in Burma's 2010 Elections', *Media, Culture & Society*, 34(5): 537–553.

Pilkington Committee on Broadcasting. (1962) *Report of the Committee on Broadcasting 1960*. London: Her Majesty's Stationery Office.

Pleming, S. (2009) 'U.S. State Department Speaks to Twitter Over Iran', URL (consulted 10 April 2012) www.reuters.com/article/2009/06/16/us-iran-election-twitter-usa-idUSWBT01137420090616.

Plunkett, J. (2012) 'Don't Break Stories on Twitter, BBC Journalists Told', URL (consulted 13 April 2012) www.guardian.co.uk/media/2012/feb/08/twitter-bbc-journalists.

Poell, T., & Borra, E. (2012) 'Twitter, YouTube, and Flickr as Platforms of Alternative Journalism: The Social Media Account of the 2010 Toronto G20 Protests', *Journalism*, 13(6): 695–713.

Potschka, C. (2012) *Towards a Market in Broadcasting: Communication Policy in the UK and Germany*. London: Palgrave Macmillan.

Reading, A. (2009) 'Mobile Witnessing: Ethics and the Camera Phone in the "War on Terror"', *Globalizations*, 6(1): 61–76.

Reese, S. (2009) 'Managing the Symbolic Arena: The Media Sociology of Herbert Gans', pp. 279–293 in L. Becker, C. Holtz-Bacha, & G. Reust (eds.), *Festschrift for Klaus Schoenbach*. Wiesbaden, VS: Verlag fuer Sozialwissenschaften.

Reese, S., Rutigliano, L., Hyun, K., & Jeong, J. (2007) 'Mapping the Blogosphere: Professional and Citizen-Based Media in the Global News Arena', *Journalism*, 8(3): 235–261.

Riegert, K., Hellman, M., Robertson, A., & Mral, B. (2010) *Transnational and National Media in Global Crisis: The Indian Ocean Tsunami*. Cresskill, NJ: Hampton Press.

Robinson, S. (2010) 'Traditionalists vs. Convergers: Textual Privilege, Boundary Work, and the Journalist-Audience Relationship in the Commenting Policies of Online News Sites', *Convergence: The International Journal of Research into New Media Technologies*, 16(1): 125–143.

Robinson, S. (2007) 'Someone's Gotta Be In Control Here: The Institutionalisation of Online News and the Creation of Shared Authority', *Journalism Practice*, 1(3): 305–321.

Rosen, J. (2006) 'The People Formerly Known as the Audience', URL (consulted April 2012) http://archive.pressthink.org/2006/06/27/ppl_frmr.html.

Roston, M., Ingber, H., Patel, S., Victor, D., Mainland, L., & Koren, S. (2013) 'If a Tweet Worked Once, Send it Again—and Other Lessons from The New York Times' Social Media Desk', URL (consulted 6 January 2014) www.niemanlab.org/2014/01/if-a-tweet-worked-once-send-it-again-and-other-lessons-from-the-new-york-times-social-media-desk.

Russell, A. (2011) *Networked: A Contemporary History of News in Transition*. Cambridge, UK: Polity Press.

Ryfe, D. M. (2012) *Can Journalism Survive? A Look at American Newsroom*. Oxford: Polity Press.

Samarajiva, R. (2005) 'Mobilizing Information and Communications Technologies for Effective Disaster Warning: Lessons from the 2004 Tsunami', *New Media & Society*, 7(6): 731–747.Sambrook, R. (2012) *Delivering Trust: Impartiality and Objectivity in the Digital Age*. Oxford: University of Oxford, Reuters Institute for the Study of Journalism.

Sambrook, R. (2010) *Are Foreign Correspondents Redundant? The Changing Face of International News*. Oxford: Reuters Institute.

Sambrook, R. (2009) 'Twittering the Uprisings?', URL (consulted 14 January 2012) http://sambrook.typepad.com/sacredfacts/2009/06/twittering-the-uprising.html.

Sambrook, R. (2005) 'Citizen Journalism and the BBC', URL (consulted 12 July 2012) www.nieman.harvard.edu/reportsitem.aspx?id=100542.

Sambrook, R. (2004) 'The Poliak Lecture Given at Columbia University, America—Holding on to Objectivity', URL (consulted 14 January 2012) www.bbc.co.uk/pressoffice/speeches/stories/sambrook_poliak.shtml.

Schlesinger, P. (1978) *Putting Reality Together: BBC News*. London: Methuen.

Schlesinger, P. (1977) 'Newsmen and their Time-Machine', *The British Journal of Sociology*, 28(3): 336–350.

Schudson, M. (2003) *The Sociology of News*. New York: W. W. Norton & Company.

Schwartzman, H. B. (1993) *Ethnography in Organizations*. Newbury Park, CA: Sage Publications.

Seib, P. (2010) 'News and Foreign Policy: Defining Influence, Balancing Power', pp. 533–541 in S. Allan (ed.), *The Routledge Companion to News and Journalism*. London: Routledge.

Settle-Blank, M. (2012) 'You Too Could be a Smartphone Reporter', URL (consulted December 2012) www.bbc.co.uk/blogs/blogcollegeofjournalism/posts/you_too_could_be_a_smartphone.

Sharma, R. (2012) 'Web Curation Tools for Journalists', URL (consulted 14 July 2012) www.bbc.co.uk/blogs/blogcollegeofjournalism/posts/web_curation_tools_for_journal.

Shiels, M. (2009) 'Twitter Responds on Iranian Role', URL (consulted 29 May 2012) http://news.bbc.co.uk/1/hi/8104318.stm.

Shirky, C. (2008) *Here Comes Everybody: The Power of Organizing Without Organizations*. New York: Penguin Press.

Sigal, L. V. (1973) *Reporters and Officials: The Organization of Politics of Newsmaking*. Lexington, MA: D.C. Health.

Simpson, J. (2002) *News From No Man's Land: Reporting the World*. London: Pan Books.

Singer, J. B. (2011) 'Journalism Ethics in a Digital Network', pp. 845–863 in R. S. Fortner & M. P. Fackler (eds.), *The Handbook of Global Communication and Media Ethics*. London: Wiley-Blackwell Publishing Ltd.

Singer, J. B. (2010) 'Quality Control', *Journalism Practice*, 4(2): 127–142.

Singer, J. B. (2005) 'The Political J-Blogger: "Normalising" a New Media Form to Fit Old Norms and Practices', *Journalism*, 6(2): 173–198.

Smith, A., Segall, L., & Cowley, S. (2012) 'Facebook Reaches One Billion Users', URL (consulted 5 March 2013) http://money.cnn.com/2012/10/04/technology/facebook-billion-users/index.html.

Soloski, J. (1989) 'News Reporting and Professionalism: Some Constraints on the Reporting of News', *Media, Culture and Society*, 11(1): 207–228.

Sonderman, J. (2011) 'BBC Social Media Policy Insists "Second Pair of Eyes" ', URL (consulted 14 January 2012) www.poynter.org/latest-news/mediawire/139412/bbc-social-media-policy-insists-second-pair-of-eyes-review-news-updates-for-twitter-or-facebook.

Stadd, A. (2013) 'Twitter: The World's Fastest-Growing Social Platform', URL (consulted 22 March 2013) www.mediabistro.com/alltwitter/twitter-growth_b36955.

Stadd, A. (2012) '20 Twitter Stats from 2012', URL (consulted 22 March 2013) www.mediabistro.com/alltwitter/twitter-stats_b32050.

Stelter, B. (2011) 'How Bin Laden Announcement Leaked Out', URL (consulted 14 January 2013) http://mediadecoder.blogs.nytimes.com/2011/05/01/how-the-osama-announcement-leaked-out/.

Stewart, D. X. (ed.). (2012) *Social Media and the Law: A Guidebook to Communication Students and Professionals.* New York: Routledge.

Strasser, F. (2012) 'Storify', URL (consulted 14 December 2012) http://franz-strasser.com/storify.

Stray, J. (2013) 'How Does a Country Get to Open Data? What Taiwan Can Teach Us About the Evolution of Access', URL (consulted 10 April 2013) www.niemanlab.org/2013/04/how-does-a-country-get-to-open-data-what-taiwan-can-teach-us-about-the-evolution-of-access/.

Stray, J. (2010) 'Drawing Out the Audience: Inside BBC's User-Generated Content Hub', URL (consulted 8 May 2012) www.niemanlab.org/2010/05/drawing-out-the-audience-inside-bbc's-user-generated-content-hub.

Stuart, C. (ed.). (1975) *The Reith Diaries.* London: Collins.

Sutcliffe, T. (2008) 'Twittering is Not the Only Way to Provide News', URL (consulted 14 January 2012) www.independent.co.uk/opinion/columnists/thomas-sutcliffe/tom-sutcliffe-twittering-on-is-not-the-way-to-provide-news-1047115.html.

Sweney, M. (2008) 'BBC Admits it Made Mistakes Using Mumbai Twitter Coverage', URL (consulted 14 January 2012) www.guardian.co.uk/media/pda/2008/dec/05/bbc-twitter.

Sweney, M. (2008b) 'BBC Restricts Staff Online Networking', URL (consulted 14 January 2012) www.guardian.co.uk/media/2008/mar/12/facebook.digitalmedia.

Sykes Committee Report. (1923) *Report of the Committee on Broadcasting.* London.

Taylor, V. (2008) 'Untitled', URL (consulted 14 January 2012) http://media.smh.com.au/technology/media-08/vicky-taylor-bbc-news-408572.html.

Thompson, M. (2005) 'Transforming the BBC—Given to the Staff', URL (consulted 14 January 2012) www.bbc.co.uk/pressoffice/speeches/stories/thompson_staff.shtml

Thurman, N. (2008) 'Forums for Citizen Journalists? Adoption of User-Generated Content Initiatives by Online News Media', *New Media & Society*, 10(1): 139–157.

Thurman, N., & Walters, A. (2013) 'Live Blogging—Digital Journalism's Pivotal Platform? A Case Study of the Production, Consumption, and Form of Live Blogs at guardian.co.uk', *Digital Journalism*, 1(1): 82–101.

Townend, J. (2009) 'BBC Director-General on Social Media Use: "You can't take BBC cloak off at will" ', URL (consulted 14 January 2012) www.journalism.co.uk/news/bbc-director-general-on-social-media-use—you-can-t-take-bbc-cloak-off-at-will-/s2/a534512.

Tuchman, G. (1978) *Making New: A Study in the Construction of Reality.* New York: Free Press.

Tuchman, G. (1974) 'Making News by Doing Work: Routinizing the Unexpected', *American Journal of Sociology*, 79(1): 110–131.

Tumber, H. (2010) 'Journalists and War Crimes', pp. 533–541 in S. Allan (ed.), *The Routledge Companion to News and Journalism.* London: Routledge.

Tunstall, J. (1971) *Journalists at Work—Specialist Correspondents: Their News Organisations, News Sources, and Competitor Colleagues.* London: Constable.

Turner, D. (2012) 'Inside the BBC's Verification Hub', URL (consulted 12 July 2012) http://nieman.harvard.edu/reportsitem.aspx?id=102764.

Turner, G. (2010) *Ordinary People and the Media: The Demotic Turn.* Los Angeles: Sage.

Turvill, W. (2013) 'Associated Press Sets Up Rangoon Bureau as Burma Opens its Doors to International Press', URL (consulted 14 January 2013) www.pressgazette.co.uk/associated-press-sets-rangoon-bureau-burma-opens-its-doors-international-press.

Usher, N. (2012) 'Marketplace Public Radio and News Routines Reconsidered: Between Structures and Agents', *Journalism*, 14(6): 807–822.

Vissens, A. (2012) 'BBC Tips for Curating Twitter Feeds—From the Russian Elections', URL (consulted 14 July 2012) www.bbc.co.uk/blogs/blogcollegeofjournalism/posts/During_the_recent_presidentia.

Waisbord, S. R. (2013) *Reinventing Professionalism: Journalism and News in Global Perspective*. Cambridge, UK: Polity.

Walton, C. (2012) 'Social Media Training is Getting Results for the BBC', URL (consulted 14 January 2012) www.bbc.co.uk/journalism/blog/2012/01/social-media-training-is-getti.shtml.

Wardle, C. (2010) 'Social Media & Journalism: A Research Critique', URL (consulted 11 June 2011) http://clairewardle.com/2010/05/23/social-media-journalism-a-research-critique.

Wardle, C. (2010b) 'The Day After—Lessons Learned From My Crowdmap Experience', URL (consulted 11 September 2010) www.bbc.co.uk/journalism/blog/2010/09/the-day-after—lessons-learne.shtml.

Wardle, C., & Williams, A. (2010) 'Beyond User-Generated Content: A Production Study Examining the Ways UGC is Used at the BBC', *Media Culture and Society*, 32(5): 781–799.

Wardle, C., & Williams, A. (2008) 'ugc@the bbc: Understanding its Impact Upon Contributors, Non-Contributors and BBC News', URL (consulted 11 June 2011) www.bbc.co.uk/blogs/knowledgeexchange/cardiffone.pdf.

Weber, M. (1981) 'Some Categories of Interpretive Sociology', *The Sociological Quarterly*, 22(2): 151–180.

Wescott, C., & Mukherjee, J. (2004) 'New Media and the BBC World Service', pp. 79–94 in C. A. Paterson & A. Sreberny (eds.), *International News in the Twenty-First Century*. London: University of Luton Press.

White, D. M. (1950) ' "The Gatekeeper": A Case Study in the Selection of News', *Journalism Quarterly*, 27(1): 383–390.

Williams, A., Wahl-Jorgensen, K., & Wardle, C. (2011) 'Studying User-Generated Content at the BBC: A Multisite Ethnography', pp. 115–128 in C. A. Paterson & D. Domingo (eds.), *Making Online News: Newsroom Ethnography in the Second Decade of Internet Journalism*. London: Peter Lang.

Williams, A., Wardle, C., & Wahl-Jorgensen, C. (2011b) ' "Have They Got News for Us?": Audience Revolution or Business as Usual at the BBC?', *Journalism Practice*, 5(1): 85–99.

Williams, J. (2012) 'Reporting Conflict in Syria', URL (consulted June 2012) www.bbc.co.uk/blogs/legacy/theeditors/2012/06/reporting_conflict_in_syria.html.

Williams, J. (2009) 'Reporting Restrictions in Iran', URL (consulted 14 January 2012) www.bbc.co.uk/blogs/theeditors/2009/06/reporting_restrictions_in_iran.html.

Williams, K. (2010) *Get Me a Murder a Day: A History of Media and Communication in Britain*, 2nd ed. London: Bloomsbury Academic.

Wolfe, A. (2008) 'Twitter In Controversial Spotlight Amid Mumbai Attacks. InformationWeek', URL (consulted 14 January 2013) www.informationweek.com/global-cio/interviews/twitter-in-controversial-spotlight-amid/229209104.

Wolfsfeld, G., Segev, E., & Sheafer, T. (2013) 'Social Media and the Arab Spring: Politics Comes First', *The International Journal of Press/Politics*, 18(2): 115–137.

Woodward, R. B. (2003) 'The 40th Anniversary of a 26-Second Reel', URL (consulted 14 January 2013) www.nytimes.com/2003/11/16/books/art-the-40th-anniversary-of-a-26-second-reel.html?pagewanted=all&src=pm.

Youngs, I. (2005) 'How ITV Changed the BBC', URL (consulted 15 July 2012) http://news.bbc.co.uk/2/hi/entertainment/4241286.stm.

Index

For Product Safety Concerns and Information please contact our EU
representative GPSR@taylorandfrancis.com
Taylor & Francis Verlag GmbH, Kaufingerstraße 24, 80331 München, Germany

www.ingramcontent.com/pod-product-compliance
Ingram Content Group UK Ltd.
Pitfield, Milton Keynes, MK11 3LW, UK
UKHW020945180425
457613UK00019B/521